CW00419971

COPYRIGHT INFORMATION

WHY MINDFULNESS IS NOT ENOUGH

-

Unlocking Compassion
with Equanimity

-

Dr Joey Weber

-

Foreword by **Professor Willem Kuyken**

"With the proliferation of interest in mindfulness over the last few years, an intelligent consideration of this phenomenon is much needed. Joey Weber's book provides just such an examination. Drawing upon Buddhist perspectives but informed by modern methods of psychological research, this book enables us to distinguish between those features of mindfulness that are truly valuable in nurturing our capacity for wisdom and compassion, and those elements which are essentially a capitulation to narcissistic consumerism."

Lama Jampa Thaye, scholar and meditation master, London

"Joey is passionate about making contemplative practice transformative not just personally, but globally. You hold in your hands one of the few books that explores the practice of equanimity with passion, depth and deep personal experience. As he states, mindfulness itself is a great step in exploring and understanding ourselves, but without understanding the importance of equanimity and compassion for ourselves and others, an important part of the jigsaw of transformation is missing. If you've tried mindfulness and want to go further into understanding both intellectually and practically where to go next, this will be a fascinating and insightful read for you."

Shamash Alidina, mindfulness teacher and author of
Mindfulness For Dummies, London

"Joey Weber shows convincingly in his pithy book that as good as mindfulness is for our wellbeing, it's even more powerful when we bring the attitude of equanimity into the mix as the foundation for the development of empathy and compassion. In other words, he shows, as the Dalai Lama points out, that our compassion not only benefits others, it benefits ourselves as well."

Robina Courtin, Buddhist teacher, Santa Fe

Contents

Dedication

I wish to dedicate this book to anyone who seeks to improve their mental wellbeing. So that probably includes just about the entirety of humanity! Furthermore, this book is dedicated to those who are committed to the ideals of self-development and the development of empathy and compassion for others.

More personally, I dedicate this book to my daughter Elodie, who taught me the need to mentally protect myself. Who knew I could love so much!

Foreword

Mindfulness provides both an understanding and a training methodology, bringing together as it does ancient and modern psychology alongside a set of mindfulness practices intended to stabilise attention, develop understanding and support a more skilful way of being and acting in the world. In this sense, mindfulness is foremost a natural, trainable human capacity. It means paying attention to whatever is happening in our minds and world in a given moment, with an attitude of interest, kindness and care. This supports our ability to see more clearly. It creates a space between our immediate experience and our immediate reactions, and that space provides a greater sense of choice, freedom and capacity to respond to life's challenges. More than this, we can see that we both literally and metaphorically create our world with our minds and hearts, moment by moment, through where we choose to place our attention and how we experience what we attend to, and through our choice of words and actions. A trained mind is better able to see clearly, make good choices, and speak and act discerningly.

Mindfulness training can be focused on particular areas and can go as far and deep as we choose. Certain mindfulness trainings emphasise focused, steady attention; others cultivate broader awareness; others develop greater understanding of how we see and understand the world; and yet others cultivate particular attitudes such as friendliness, compassion, joy or equanimity. Each of these can be tasted or developed systematically in quite profound and transformative ways. All together, these elements of mindfulness support a sense of common humanity and confidence that we have the capacity to respond with greater discernment at challenging times; that, somehow, within us, we can find peace in the midst of great difficulty.

This work pivots on our ability to keep a cool head and warm heart – in short, this is equanimity, or, stated more simply, balance. This can seem a simple idea, and in some ways it is. But, when we reflect on our minds and behaviours, we soon realise that it is an advanced skill and practice. In secular mindfulness it is also an idea that receives less attention than some of the other facets of mindfulness.

This book redresses this and puts equanimity front and centre. It is comprehensive and carefully structured, considering both the individual but also the wider world – and the way equanimity can support wellbeing at both of these levels. It provides practical ways that equanimity can be cultivated, including practices readers can use. Dr Weber is well-placed to write this book, writing as he does based on both his research programme and his personal embodied mindfulness practice.

Willem Kuyken
Ritblat Professor of Mindfulness and Psychological Science,
University of Oxford

Introduction

The explosion of mindfulness as a Western practice has put 'being present' on the map. *Mindfulness* is generally defined as the awareness that arises through paying attention on purpose, in the present moment, non-judgementally.[1] You can now find an abundance of mindfulness-based wellbeing initiatives that are accessible to everyone, whether individually, through healthcare services or through the workplace. This undoubtedly serves as a wonderful counter-narrative in a world often entrenched in competitive individualism fuelled with high anxiety and mental neurosis.

As a Western child being brought up with a strong dash of Tibetan Mahayana Buddhism, I consider myself to have a unique vantage point for exploring the intricacies of mindfulness and its proponents for a wellbeing revolution. Like a glass of water with added cordial, the lens of my experience is coloured with ideas of self-transformation and universal compassion. Indeed, in order to explore the potential of an even greater mark on a wellbeing revolution, my research focuses on the construct of equanimity, which I will show to be an essential element of mindfulness.

Equanimity is the non-reactivity of one's own discrimination faculties (categorisation into likes, dislikes and neutralities), so you can monitor your own responses with compassion for yourself and others. There is both an inner and outer equanimity, which I define in greater detail in Chapter 2. Equanimity propels mindfulness into a more robust arena and is of equal importance for creating a more harmonious society. Essentially, if we develop equanimity, this will lead to a more compassionate society, because it will reduce bias and strengthen social cohesion. This is because equanimity brings a heightened sense of awareness towards our own biases and, in doing so, makes unconscious bias conscious. This leads us to act with more compassion towards ourselves and others. We become able to accept other people's bias with greater compassion. In facilitating this inner and outer process, equanimity binds society together as a more cohesive whole.

Contemporary mindfulness practice can increase selfishness if we don't also examine our *sense of self* – who we are, which I talk about in

---

1 Mindful Staff (2017) Jon Kabat-Zinn: Defining Mindfulness. Available at: www. mindful.org/jon-kabat-zinn.

Chapter 3 – in relation to our motivation for becoming more mindful. And although equanimity is implicitly taught in mindfulness, if we were to pay more attention to equanimity then we may be able to mitigate the potential shortcomings of the contemporary 'popular mindfulness' movement (I explore these issues in Chapter 1).

Exploring Barriers to Equanimity

This book offers an exploration of equanimity, as well as a model of how we form judgements (Chapter 4) that helps us to understand our barriers to equanimity. Chapter 5 shares a psychometric scale that can capture and explore personal barriers to equanimity.

Mindfulness and meditation do not yield the same results for everyone; indeed, there are some examples of mindfulness causing distress for people.[2] Therefore, exploring why we think and behave the way we do relies on a closer inspection of our own unique mental discrimination faculties.

By exploring the barriers to equanimity, it is possible to examine why some people find mindfulness more difficult than others, as well as offer an explanation into the different ways that people practise mindfulness meditation and the underlying reasons why mindfulness can be so effective for people. Equanimity enhances the efficacy of *mindfulness-based interventions* (mindfulness programmes such as mindfulness-based stress reduction and mindfulness-based cognitive therapy), because it improves the ability for mindfulness to be successful by narrowing in on the aspects of non-judgement, acceptance and curiosity. Only by understanding what makes mindfulness so effective are we able to accurately assess our individual growth and potential for transformation. (*Transformation*, in this context, being the improvement and eventual subsiding of the mental disharmony we experience from our own inner voices, plus any additional disharmony in relationships.)

From a scientific perspective, it is difficult to assess the value of mindfulness-based interventions without the clarity of equanimity. Without a clear emphasis on equanimity, mindfulness teachings may lack quality control and the meditations may not venture into the

---

2 Finucane, A. and Mercer, S.W. (2006) An exploratory mixed methods study of the acceptability and effectiveness of mindfulness-based cognitive therapy for patients with active depression and anxiety in primary care. *BMC Psychiatry*, 6(1), 14.

realms of compassion as much as they could. If the intention of the mindfulness-based intervention is to enable more prosocial activities, such as developing empathy or compassion, then it would be remiss to overlook equanimity. Furthermore, because of the lack of emphasis on equanimity, current research tools designed to measure the value of a particular mindfulness-based intervention fail to capture this essential ingredient. For example, a study may measure its participants effectively in terms of attention or focus, but it may be less effective at measuring non-judgement or experiential acceptance.

I outline a seven-step process in Chapter 6 to help anyone to develop an equanimity mindset. I also share some sample meditations to try, as well as some case studies that bring equanimity to life. The case studies are particularly valuable because they outline how we can apply equanimity on a day-to-day basis, instead of simply reading about it. Like anything, merely describing the taste of something is not the same as actually eating it and finding out for yourself!

Understanding Our 'Inner Capitalist'

In the context of a world "forever chasing happiness, hoping to find it in the forgetfulness of pleasure,"[3] mindfulness can be twisted to be used as a tool for enhancing the egos of the frustrated and insecure. For example, if an individual engages with mindfulness from a self-centred perspective, then mindfulness might only amplify that individual's ego. But this is still a necessary first step. Everyone starts by wanting happiness for themselves, but then they have the opportunity to develop their understanding and discover how mindful psychology really works.

More so than ever before, we are sold the promise of happiness so powerfully, and yet so often we only encounter discontent. Believe it or not, this natural human reaction stems from the sheer simplicity of an individual's sense of what they like, what they dislike, and what they find neutral. In the age of social media and 'fake news', equanimity is fundamental for restoring peace and balance because it amplifies our inner truths.

This book is pertinent to you if you are an *inner capitalist*. By this, I don't mean someone who follows capitalism's external political and

3 Thaye, L.J. (2017) *Wisdom in Exile: Buddhism and Modern Times*, Dechen Foundation.

ideological doctrines. Instead, I mean that you wish to accumulate happiness and you suffer from an unquenchable and unequivocal desire for pleasure – you not only go out of your way to experience pleasure, but also to avoid pain or unhappiness (for example, you may go to the nearest open shop at midnight to buy chocolate, but also try to delay doing the washing up or avoid having difficult conversations!). By this metric, aren't we all just trying to get to the top of the happiness pile? Aren't we all inner capitalists?

For this theory to be tested, we must look towards our own minds: the mind that discriminates into categories in order to make sense of and to understand an object (the object being either sensory, a thought or a material object, or a person). Like a great white shark with a droplet of blood in the ocean, we swim towards pleasure at a rapid pace, as if a trance-like gravitational pull is drawing us towards the object of our desire. If we like it, we want more of it; if we don't like it, we become averse to it; if we find it neutral, we don't give it much attention. We all gravitate towards the things we like and want more and more of them, in the hope they will make us happy. If it tastes good, we want to consume more; if it sounds nice, we want to continue listening. Whatever experiences we don't like, we try to avoid them or react emotionally, instead of thoughtfully responding. That is, in essence, a simple way of explaining our discriminating minds. Our quest for what we like can drive how we choose to live our lives.

Tibetan Buddhist nun Robina Courtin once told me, *"We are just sense junkies, desperate to cling on to what gives us pleasure and doing whatever it takes to give us pleasure."* When we don't get what we want, the toys are thrown out of the pram, and the ego recoils and finds a way to protect itself, either by pretending it didn't want it much in the first place, suppressing the feelings, manipulating the situation to feel a sense of victory, or simply feeling frustration or anger.

Many virtuous leaders and philosophers remind us that we share the same underlying desires; the wish to be happy and free from suffering. Although our understanding of suffering may differ slightly between cultures, we can all relate to this sense of discontent, frustration or psychological distress. In this way, we are one huge human family with the wish to be as happy as possible, and we are constantly striving to make this happen. If we change the word 'happiness' to 'wealth', our minds can be understood to have this acquiring nature to want more and more of the good stuff (to be an inner capitalist). When we practice equanimity, it enables us to engage with our inner capitalist and become less driven by desire, more wise and compassionate, and, ultimately, more content.

A Socially Aware and Mindful Revolution

The reasons for examining equanimity and its promotion of compassion seem ever more pressing in an often polarised world, with wars on terror, a global pandemic, Brexit and vast political unrest influencing our mental health and how we live our lives. For example, social commentators cast aspersions against scientists, and as a result we can see a rapid growth of fake news and a looming distrust of experts (even the word 'expert', which used to symbolise the pinnacle of knowledge, now seems to have become another adjective for a mere position or political point of view). The COVID-19 pandemic has shone a bright light on the stark realities that may face us as a planet. Yet, for some, this has only stirred the embers for a wider discursive divisiveness. Naming and shaming seems to be an accepted and advocated part of our media, and it is not uncommon to either become emotionally enraged or to withdraw from someone due to their comments on social media. Public outcries typically take a broad-brush approach to complex scenarios, which undermines the context underlying many challenging issues.

As an example, consider high-profile crimes. It seems there is little public-facing analysis or understanding of the psychological workings of the mind of a person who commits a crime; instead, the focus may shift towards anger, lack of empathy or an inability to manage deep-rooted feelings of hatred. If we pay more attention to the ways in which we respond, rather than fanning the flames of anger or rage in the moment, then perhaps we may increase our compassion and reduce the likelihood of future crimes. It is not that criminal acts should not receive justice, but more that it might be helpful to engage in deeper discussions that could shed light on the reasons why criminal behaviour occurs. A collective experience of rage may take the place of any learning or insight that might result from the situation. Ultimately, we inflict more suffering onto ourselves through our feelings of anger. To paraphrase a quote generally attributed to the Buddha, we pick up the hot coal and throw it, burning ourselves in the process. However, if we were to respond with equanimity, we would remain steadfast in our desire for justice, while our approach would be calm. Equanimity enables us to be objective and less likely to personalise a difficult experience.

Politics seems to have positioned itself at the heart of the wellbeing revolution, so the ethics of mindfulness-based interventions must be made more explicit. Non-judgement and acceptance can mean different things to different people, and while focus and attention are apolitical, non-judgement and acceptance are clearly not because they directly relate to bias. Some feel that political ideology is at the heart of the converging crises of the 21st century (such as climate change and widening inequality). This is because policies may be seen to ramp up the costs of wellbeing initiatives, reduce mental health services and create wider inequalities between the state of a nation's mental health by minimising inclusion. It may also reduce the concept of wellbeing to a monetised product available at a fee for the privileged few.

Mindfulness and equanimity can influence how we behave in a socio-political context given their ability to enhance compassion (explored further in Chapter 7). And for those who believe we are too far gone, that there can be no systemic change, then at least mindfulness can support them in their quest for personal and local change. There is after all no way of telling what mindfulness may do for a person, what resonates with them and what this may lead to. I also align to the opinion that it asks an awful lot of mindfulness to elicit social change! After all, modern-day mindfulness began life in a secular way as a form of stress reduction and made no attempts at proclaiming it would become the new world order.

However, if we limit the discussion to this, I fear that we are opting for safety and not pushing our human potential to its limits to truly generate change. Thus, by placing mindfulness and equanimity at the heart of the debate, social activism can take on a new approach. At present, mindfulness could in fact reinforce control-seeking behaviours and narcissism, because one might pursue mindfulness with ignorance (regarding the ethical motivation behind its practice), a lack of awareness about one's own biases, prejudices and habitual ways of being, and a lack of curiosity about one's own sense of self. In this way, mindfulness as it stands does not always nurture the multi-perspectives required for interacting with others and relaxing around their efforts, because it largely ignores the role of our biases, our discrimination faculties and compassion. This will be explored further in Chapter 1.

The idea of a compassionate world view is becoming increasingly commonplace, with the need for global unification (for example, with regard to climate change) being propagated by a variety of social commentators. Human beings will disagree with one another, which is natural, but how we disagree and react to this disharmony does not need to lead to the kind of discontent that compromises our ability to act compassionately. So perhaps a mindful revolution can begin by embracing diversity and finding ways to agree to disagree with harmony, from the base notes of awareness: a revolution set on tending to and caring for the moment in a bid to transcend autopilot and swim in a sea of peaceful particles that satisfies everyone's sensitivities.

What You Can Expect from This Book

I wrote this book with the hope that it can improve mental wellbeing individually and collectively. But reading this book may simply not be enough to help you. At most, reading it may reveal some rigid boundaries in your thinking, your view of yourself or your view of wellbeing. But, for real change, we must also put things into practice. It is not enough to be able to describe equanimity; we need to experience it and we have to apply the method. It is the same with meditation: we need to understand why, what and how to do it, but ultimately we need to practise it. Driving tests are the same. We do the theory before we attempt the practical. Experiencing equanimity becomes the balance of the theory and the practical.

With equanimity, we embark on our quest for self-development with greater rigour. In essence, we extend our introspective toolkit. Hopefully, by the end of the book, your mind will be receptive enough to put equanimity into practice and to experience the many benefits of an equanimous mindset.

Chapter 1: Expanding the Limits of Mindfulness with Equanimity

Mindfulness is now ingrained on the consciousness of the masses. Even if someone is not a mindfulness practitioner, it is not uncommon for them to have at least read an article or come across mindfulness in passing.

As Jon Kabat-Zinn's famous definition reminds us, mindfulness is about paying attention on purpose, in the present moment, non-judgementally.[4] Mindfulness is not about being spaced out and being submerged in the dreamlike nature of thought; instead, it is as if we have emerged fresh-faced after a cold splash of water. It's all about present-moment awareness.

However, the simple mantra of 'awareness, awareness, awareness' has far more to it than has penetrated our public perception. Perhaps the mindfulness faultfinders use this simplicity to criticise it. Somehow, straightforwardness and ease act as a barrier to the intellectual mind, which is so used to analytical appraisal and a positioned stance. The cynic in me can hear the tick-box-loving CEOs now: "Let us give them a day of wellbeing and tell them to grab a 'breath of fresh air' and then we can put mindfulness back into its box and concentrate on efficiency and effectiveness." This attitude has led critics to brand it 'McMindfulness'.[5] My question is, have we got good reason to feel cynical? Has mindfulness branded itself too successfully as accessible and easy to achieve, making mindful wellbeing difficult to respect and take seriously?

I hope not. I believe that mindfulness has a lot to offer our society, our health and our personal lives. Compassion is another integral element of mindful living. There is a place for equanimity to step onto the chariot of mindfulness: not to push mindfulness out of the way and take the reins, but to complement it and gently steer it in a more compassionate direction.

A Brief History of Mindfulness

Thich Nhat Hanh, a Vietnamese Buddhist monk and social/peace activist, is one of the world's pioneers of mindfulness and is often credited with

---

4 Kabat-Zinn, J. (2005) *Wherever You Go, There You Are: Mindfulness Meditation in Everyday Life*, Hachette Books.
5 Purser, R. (2019) *McMindfulness*, Repeater Books.

bringing mindfulness (and Buddhism) to the West. He famously coined the term 'engaged Buddhism', and he has since founded organisations and monasteries aimed at cultivating peace and encouraging mindful living. In 1967, Martin Luther King Jr. nominated Thich Nhat Hanh for a Nobel Peace Prize. In 1982, Hanh founded Plum Village in southern France, one of the West's most active Buddhist monasteries with over 200 resident monks and nuns and up to 8,000 visitors every year. His writings, poems and spiritual leadership continue to be globally influential in the 21st century.[6]

In 1979, Jon Kabat-Zinn (one of Thich Nhat Hanh's students) developed the mindfulness-based stress reduction (MBSR) programme at the University of Massachusetts Medical Center. While there is acknowledgement that MBSR has Buddhist influences (as mindfulness sits at the heart of Buddhism), the programme is secular and non-religious. The programme originated during a vipassana (insight) retreat, when Jon had a vision that his 13 years of experience in meditation and yoga could somehow find its way into American hospital corridors. He believed that this combination could evolve into something deeply transformative. It was thanks to this vision that he developed the MBSR programme, which led to the creation of the world's first mindfulness-based stress reduction clinic.

The whole point behind MBSR was to recontextualise the teachings of the Buddha within the framework of science, medicine and healthcare for people who would otherwise not be aware of MBSR or able to access it. Kabat-Zinn thought that the term 'meditation' could develop its own meaning over time, one that went beyond Buddhism – not because its culture or history was not important, but because the religious association with the term might create an unnecessary obstruction for people who were suffering and who would benefit from mindfulness meditation. What better place than a hospital to make meditation available to people who may benefit from it as a complement to more traditional treatments?

The model gradually evolved in the 90s into what we know today as the MBSR eight-week programme, which teaches those with various conditions (such as chronic pain, depression and anxiety) how they can use mindfulness meditation to manage their individual circumstances. Since

6 Plum Village (Not dated) The Life Story of Thich Nhat Hanh. Available at: https://plumvillage.org/about/thich-nhat-hanh/biography/.

the 90s, thousands of people have completed the programme, and there are now hundreds of MBSR courses across the globe that are modelled on Kabat-Zinn's original programme. Scientific evidence reinforces how mindfulness has positive effects on varied health and psychological benefits, such as improved physical and mental health and psychological wellbeing. As a result of Jon Kabat-Zinn's work, as well as the work of countless researchers in recent decades, today the term 'meditation' is commonly understood and accepted in Western civilisation.[7]

Mindfulness Is a Lifelong Journey, Not a Panacea

One common misconception is that once you have found mindfulness, you are 'cured'. However, mindfulness is only really effective if it is a continued journey (rather than a momentary experiment with meditation that is not integrated into our lives in a more embodied way of living).

Take the theatre as a metaphor. Imagine that the show is your neurotic mind and the awareness is a rather refreshing interval. Mindfulness is often portrayed rather one-dimensionally because it is perceived that the 'interval' is enough. In reality, this metaphor does not work as, of course, a break from the show just allows a new 'play' to ensue – this one I imagine to involve ice cream, a bit of a chat and a check of the phone. But self-help books, social media and the abundance of guru figures seem to suggest that once you have experienced the tantalising seduction of awareness, then you have found the path to freedom and there is just no turning back. Just ten minutes of mindfulness a day and you will literally be the happiest person alive, with no worries or stresses for the rest of your life. We celebrate the interval as if it is enough. However, if the interval is a brief moment of awareness, of stillness, of simply being that is conjured up as a step back from our neurotic play, then our mind will resume its neuroticism fairly swiftly.

In Buddhism, the mind is often likened to an unruly elephant that is prone to wandering away from the path towards enlightenment. The elephant is symbolic of mental strength; however, before its training it erratically demolishes everything in its path. Our minds are like the elephant before its training; they are briefly tamed with mindfulness, then they continue to behave erratically. By taming the elephant over

7 Kabat-Zinn, J. (2011) Some reflections on the origins of MBSR, skillful means, and the trouble with maps. *Contemporary Buddhism*, 12(1), 281–306.

time, we strengthen its ability for patience and tranquillity; likewise, if we train our minds over time, they become loyal and responsible. However, this is not a quick fix.

Mindfulness is a lifelong quest. A Tibetan depiction of the Shamatha (tranquillity) meditation (which includes a variety of mind-calming techniques, the most common being mindfulness of breathing, with a goal of being able to concentrate on a single point without distraction) does an incredible job of showing the complexities an individual embarks on from the point of first coming into contact with meditation, as shown in Figure 1.1.

A series of monk figures (with a hook of introspection and a rope of mindfulness) gradually move from focusing the elephant's mind on an object (and then maintaining the elephant's mind's focus on the object) through to stronger introspection, until a person enters single-pointed concentration and experiences a tranquil mind. As the monk begins the path, there are specific stages of mind control to accomplish by applying the mental power of memory (rope) and alertness (taming hook). The monk begins his journey – starting with an untrained elephant mind, and served only by the monkey of distraction – then gradually sets about implementing the correct methods to finally realise single-pointed concentration (represented by the flaming sword).

Figure 1.1: Andy Weber Studios (Calm Abiding/Shamatha, available at:
https://andyweberstudios.com/product/calm-abiding-shamatha/).

Mindfulness is 'concentration plus'. As we delve into attention via the breath or the subtle feelings of the body, we begin a new relationship with concentration. From concentration, we facilitate our capacity for awareness. It is perhaps pertinent to say that Shamatha (or total tranquillity, calmness and single-pointed concentration) is the 'end goal' of mindfulness (if anyone would be brazen enough to say there is an end goal of mindfulness!). Over time, we gain greater mental stability and a greater experience of inner calm.

The paradox of our age is that we have an abundance of scientifically proven contemplative magic available at our fingertips, but also an abundance of things that serve only to distract us (represented by the monkey of distraction in Figure 1.1). Indeed, the entirety of social media serves as a distraction-based economy, which advertisers have built around our tendency to be frivolous with our attention. We feed the belly of the beast of distraction, then we feel confused by how empty we feel inside. Therefore, inner awareness and balance become even more important.

How can we balance the wish for personal transformation against a Netflix account with thousands of programmes accessible within seconds? Why should we meditate when we can 'watch-itate'? The answer is pure and simple but definitely not easy – and it requires an enthusiasm for and dedication to self-improvement.

Mindfulness is rewarding but it can be hard work; however, it is because of my love for mindfulness that I feel compelled to nurture it further by researching around mindfulness and seeking to deepen our understanding of it. For all of its shortcomings and potential pitfalls, mindfulness has improved thousands of lives and will continue to do so as it acts as a buffer for our neurotic mental health in the 21st century.

The Popularity Paradox

When a term becomes so commonplace that it's mentioned in workplace corridors, on playgrounds or in bars, it can lose its depth of meaning due to the myriad ways in which each person may have arrived at their own unique version of the term. To paraphrase Theodore Zeldin: for any new food or custom to be accepted by a society, it must add some of its own flavours to conceal the exoticness from itself.[8] Maybe mindfulness was a perfect new dish when it arrived on the contemporary scene. But might

---

8 Zeldin, T. (2011) *An Intimate History of Humanity*, Vintage Books.

some of its essence have been lost in the inevitable upscaling and rolling out of its flavours on a larger scale?

There is plenty of evidence-based science behind mindfulness, so we understand that there is more to it than the simple notion of 'following the breath' (or mindfully eating a grape or having a mindful shower). The evidence base for the benefits of mindfulness, from randomised controlled trials[9] to smaller qualitative explorations,[10] covers everything from managing chronic illness, anxiety and depression[11] to enhancing creativity and reducing the effects of ageing.[12]

Indeed, I align with Jon Kabat-Zinn's view that mindfulness is for everyone from all walks of life, across the entire political spectrum and from all religious backgrounds. Mindfulness has an extraordinary reach due to its boundaryless nature. However, it would be foolish to think it can withstand corruptibility or the potential to be misinterpreted or misunderstood.

What Makes Mindfulness Seem Selfish?

For those not yet sold on the idea that mindfulness can be transformative, or for those who believe it is merely an intellectual exercise about focusing on the present moment, mindfulness could be stereotyped as a rather overindulgent, selfish activity; however, it is far from that simple. Where else do you step out of thought and into awareness, accepting things non-judgementally in order to approach any given situation with full presence, tenderness and care? Where else do you begin to examine and question the very nature of self and explore the quality of your own presence?

However, mindfulness often falls short of the true meaning of self-transformation, given that one of the key elements of mindfulness is to be non-judgemental. The open willingness to fully examine the self in

9 Goldberg, S, Tucker, R, Greene, P, Davidson, R, Wampold, B, Kearney, D and Simpson, T (2018) Mindfulness-based interventions for psychiatric disorders: A systematic review and meta-analysis, *Clinical Psychology Review*, 59: 52-60

10 Nickerson, A. and Hinton, D. (2011) Anger regulation in traumatized Cambodian refugees: The perspectives of Buddhist monks. *Culture Medicine and Psychiatry*, 35(3): 396–416.

11 Hofmann, S.G., Sawyer, A.T., Witt, A.A. and Oh, D. (2010) The effect of mindfulness-based therapy on anxiety and depression: A meta-analytic review. *Journal of Consulting and Clinical Psychology*, 78(2), 169–183.

12 Luders, E. (2014) Exploring age-related brain degeneration in meditation practitioners. *Annals of the New York Academy of Sciences*, 1307, 82–88.

any given moment and reach into the heart of your mind and the mind of your heart is often too subtly imbalanced (given mindfulness's lack of true introspection) because of a misunderstanding of the term 'non-judgement' (explored in more detail later in this section).

This lack of introspection can be redressed with equanimity; without it, mindfulness runs the risk of being reduced down to another commodity. Because of the consumerist way of life, and the mantra of efficiency and effectiveness, there is the risk of exploitation and the need to get things done quickly. We may want a quick fix rather than taking the time to find a lasting solution, which is why we might decide that doing a weekend course is enough and yet question why meditating once a month doesn't bring us lasting peace. Or perhaps we simply wait for a crisis in our lives before we turn to meditation and mindfulness.

We need to unpick the very attributes that could make mindfulness without equanimity quite a selfish pursuit:

> Acceptance
> Attention
> Non-judgement
> Awareness

These attributes very much take the person at their own unique starting point and do not imply any form of self-analysis. But if the world view of a person is faulty (that is, if their motivation is not ethically driven), then despite being mindful, the world view of the person remains the same. If someone's bias is so ingrained, then during less mindful moments they will still be afflicted by their own bias. If a person can be mindful and yet pursue greed or hate, can we still call them mindful?

Acceptance

Accepting things that hurt us, or accepting things in a way that closely resembles suppression, repression or denial, is a misguided form of acceptance. If we train ourselves to accept everything, then we do not give things the deeper analysis they deserve. Perhaps superficial acceptance or surface-level acceptance is better suited to describe the ways in which 'acceptance of all' sits within mindfulness. That is, we accept things without understanding the basis of our judgement and what our judgement means.

While acceptance may not seem overly selfish, *unexamined* acceptance can be – in other words, blindly accepting what is said by others or by your own self-talk without any form of insight or inquiry. Acceptance relies on the premise that what is said can be accepted without emotional harm. Yet, not everything that occurs is unfortunately without harm, given what life can throw at us, such as grief, conflict or sadness. Thus, there needs to be tender, heartfelt examination when it comes to acceptance.

Acceptance does not have to come without a fight for a worthy cause. We can accept things and still fight them. This leans more towards equanimity. Suppose someone makes a rude comment on our social media. With equanimity, we allow the event to sit with us while we monitor our emotions or thoughts. Then we accept the event that has taken place, before we decide with wisdom how to respond (for example, to respond constructively or let it go). Think about using acceptance as a way to help you rather than as a passive activity, which in turn can allow you to deal with an issue without emotional upheaval. This turns acceptance more towards equanimity by dissecting what it truly means to accept. I focus on this more in Chapter 6.

Attention

Attention can be totally selfish because it is the 'I' (our self-construct) that chooses what we pay attention to. In mindfulness, it is the motivation behind where we place our attention that becomes the most interesting thing. This relies on awareness but is intrinsically connected to the idea of the 'self' (I explore the notion of the self more in Chapter 3). Typically, the self will consider the best alternatives and then home in on an object of attention that gives the individual the most pleasure. The self will not choose to focus on the negatives or the neutrals. Why? There is no reward there. Therefore, unless we connect our deepest motivations with compassion, our attention flag will be hard to stick in the ground. The flag of attention will be pulled from pillar to post with the distracted wind of the mind, and when it seeks and finds the fertile ground that gives it pleasure, only then will it take root. Yet, when this pleasure goes, the attention too will go. So, a deepening connection with motivation and compassion for others is needed in order to ensure you are trying to at least put the flag in the right general area! If you don't address your motivation and compassion for others, then you run the risk of using the attention created through mindfulness to garner more things that do not truly give you satisfaction. The grasping nature of the self will be leading the hunt, and only the pleasurable sense objects – that are never enough – will be the self's prey.

With attention, we are at risk of exaggerating the qualities of an object and becoming attached to them, since we oscillate around pleasurable sensory objects. This is pretty much how the roots of addiction are formed.

Thus, equanimity tempers the 'selfishness' of attention because it gives you a compassionate focus; that is, looking beyond the self.

Non-judgement

The social world is designed to play on your likes and dislikes; for example, hedonism is dependent upon you liking something enough to want to buy it and own it. Fake news is designed to play on the heartstrings of the judgemental in order to sell products and services and receive clicks. In fact, most news directly plays into a moralising arena for good/bad, right/wrong and love/detest. The entire eight billion of us are ready to spring forth with our own version of events, offer our opinions and revel in our own discrimination.

Judgements are communicated, debated and assigned followers, rejecters or people who find it all indifferent. These both happen to us and because of us at every given moment. In short, the cyclical effects of judgements tie us and those around us to our sense of self and vice versa. Thus, our judgements are entirely selfish.

When we hear of the rather angelic concept of non-judgement, we may immediately believe ourselves to already live like this. However, recent studies[13] on inherent racism highlight how our unconscious minds are altered by perceived groupings: differences in skin colour, ethnicity, weight, height or perceived attractiveness, for example. The truth is, we categorise by nature and cannot escape this. So, to be 'non-judgemental' is to playfully sign ourselves up to this value without any real conviction. Yet how are we genuinely practising it? How do we become non-judgemental when we categorise and judge things on a second-by-second basis? In short, we can become non-judgemental by fostering equanimity, but this is by no means a quick solution. This involves directly analysing the self over the course of a lifetime. Chapter 4 is all about dealing with

---

13 BBC (2019) Implicit bias: Is everyone racist? Available at: https://www.bbc.com/news/magazine-40124781.

judgements with the help of equanimity.

Awareness

Awareness of what? Awareness of how to please the self more, or how to be more compassionate towards others? Awareness of the self is paramount to mindfulness. We do not heighten our awareness so that our feelings become intensified; instead, we heighten our awareness so we can act from wisdom. However, we can never be too sure, such is the subtle gravitational pull of indulgence, self-satisfaction, desire and hedonism. As your ability to be mindful grows, so you grow your sprig of awareness into an ivy of compassion, allowing the intention to seep into each and every crevice of your being. With the wisdom of equanimity, our awareness is not merely showing us how to get what we want for ourselves, but how we can extend our compassion for the benefit of the many.

Moving Towards Compassion for Yourself and Others

For me, the concept that truly binds mindfulness with compassion is equanimity. This chapter has highlighted how, without introspection, mindfulness can become selfish and oversimplified, and simply reinforce maladaptive behaviours. With greater introspection, equanimity can aid the skills of acceptance, attention, non-judgement and awareness by moving mindfulness beyond selfishness and towards compassion for yourself and others. Equanimity steers mindfulness in a healthier direction, avoiding the perils of misinterpretation, misunderstanding and unethical practice.

Takeaway Points:

> Mindfulness is scientifically proven to be amazing!
> Mindfulness is a journey, not a quick fix.
> The mainstream appeal of mindfulness opens it up to misunderstanding and unfair criticism, which means mindfulness may be misinterpreted at a large scale.
> Without equanimity, mindfulness can become too diluted and selfish.
> A key element that binds mindfulness with compassion is equanimity.

Chapter 2: Introducing Equanimity

Equanimity is the embrace between insight and love.

With mindfulness, you get up close and personal with the present moment. You are non-judgemental and accepting. You exist with the raw nakedness of what is happening in the moment. But with equanimity, you deepen that closeness to the present moment even further, with sustained compassion for yourself and others, fully aware of your own experience.

There is a sense in the mindfulness community that everyone knows what equanimity is. I know I make it sound pretty amazing here, so surely everyone would know all about it! However, as I started to research equanimity, I realised that it had been overlooked. In fact, the term was relatively obsolete, and I discovered that terms like 'non-judgement' and 'de-centering' were the closest terms to describe equanimity. There was no body of knowledge that held equanimity under a microscope and so, because of its different contextual meanings, it could mean different things in both research and practice.

This has several implications, such as the potential for misinterpretation and a misunderstanding of equanimity's relevance in modern-day mindfulness-based interventions. Further, it could mean that mindfulness-based interventions may not spend a significant amount of time working on developing equanimity, and practitioners may also be missing out on developing their understanding of this crucial element of mindfulness.

In this chapter, I take a deep dive into what equanimity is and how it can make all the difference to our experience of mindfulness. I also consider some of the misconceptions about equanimity that I have encountered while researching this fascinating subject.

The Discriminatory Mind

Based on my extensive reading, I compiled the following two-part definition of equanimity, which has both an inner and outer quality:

> (i) Inner equanimity – Open acceptance of non-reactivity towards our own discrimination faculties (pleasure, displeasure, neutrality), so we can respond with compassion for self and others.

(ii) External equanimity – Accepting another individual's discrimination faculties (pleasure, displeasure, neutrality) with patience, so as to respond with compassion for self and others.[14]

In order to understand equanimity, we need to become familiar with the discriminatory mind. The way we see the world is through three main lenses: we discriminate between what we like, what we dislike and what we find neutral. This introduces us to the basic premise of equanimity: that our minds are continually judging, even on an unconscious level. Try out the discriminative mind test to see what I mean!

The discriminative mind test:

1. In your mind, right now, what things are you thinking of? Write them down. (Alternatively, make a list of the first ten things you see around you.)
2. Look at these things more objectively. Can you distinguish them into categories: the things you like, dislike and find neutral?
3. Consider to what lengths you gravitate towards the people, places or objects that bring you happiness or pleasure.

Our minds are continually and relentlessly discriminating between what we like, do not like or find neutral. The discriminative mind test gives us an initial snapshot of how our mind works to categorise our experiences. It shows how often we may gravitate towards pleasure without even noticing it. Look around you. You may notice objects that you are particularly drawn to over others, maybe because of particular colours, textures or comfort, such as the sofa. Perhaps there are objects that you are neutral towards, such as the wallpaper, the shelves or the bookcase. Then there may be things that you do not like, such as an imperfection in the bookcase, the smell of the carpet or a chip in an ornament.

Equanimity requires us to start heightening our awareness towards our own categorisations, recognising that these categories fuel the majority of our thoughts, emotions and behaviour. These categories (such as pleasure/displeasure, good/bad and right/wrong) can easily lead us towards more polarised views, acting as kindling to an unlit fire.

What may start off as harmless distaste could quickly become an

14 Weber, J. (2019) Operationalising equanimity in clinical practice: A mindful approach. Clinical Psychology Forum, October edition.

unshakable point of view. What we like lights up what we find pleasurable and then, if we become over-attached to this object, we want more and more of it. Then we are frustrated if we can't have it. What we dislike gives rise to displeasure and we become averse to it, reject and criticise it Then we are frustrated that we have to live with it. And all those mid-level feelings – the neutralities –just become forgotten or put in the 'dislike' pile because they don't titillate us. This behaviour isn't actually helpful. Why? Because these things are all linked to our sense of self, which is not always wired up in the healthiest way. How many of us are completely free from some form of past trauma from our childhood, relationships or career and have the courage to look inside ourselves in order to grow as people? Our sense of self usually carries with it years' worth of baggage; of things not going the way we wanted, relationships failing, employment going wrong or arguments with family members. We need to become more honest with who we are.

If something doesn't ignite our interest, then often we overlook things that are neutral. But, in life, it is the neutral things that make up the majority of our experience. You can check this out now by reviewing what happened to you yesterday. How much of it do you remember? I would guess that you only remember the few parts that were enjoyable or caused you some distress. But you were alive for a full day. Why is it that we only remember the polarised times? Because the others were all categorised as neutral! The little things in life are actually the big things. We just take them for granted and overlook most of our daily experiences as unimportant because they either do not inspire us or cause us distaste. But if we live like that, then most of life is like living in a waiting room, waiting for the next big thing to make us happy. What if it never comes? Now might be a good time to go and find joy in the wallpaper!

We limit ourselves with our own rigid categorisations. We place prison-like internal walls over every subjective experience. We thought our judgements were giving us sense and meaning, the ability to analyse and survive, but it turns out our discriminative minds have been placing limiting boundaries upon everything. We have gone beyond survival mode. Now is the time to flourish. One person's neutral is another person's joy; one person's like is another's dislike. We need to remember that our opinions are 'our' truth so it may be right for us but not others, and if we remain stuck in our judgements then divisiveness with others can ensue. Views can quickly become polarising and we then live by our categorisations and define ourselves by them. In fact, if we are not aware of our own categories then we are living quite small lives. Or we relate to others in ways that restrict their autonomy. Finding equanimity in everything is like standing at the precipice of openness.

The Self-centred 'I'

When we grasp on to what we like and reject what we don't like, or we find dullness in the neutral, we are living in a self-centred way. But imagine how different our lives would look if we could extend the parameters of our compassion to the people we find boring, tedious or annoying! Or even to those who we dislike. Or we were able to find joy in the little things, even happiness when things do not go our way. This is the antidote to divisiveness, which is one of the biggest problems in society right now. How long before we are swept off our own feet because of what is happening outside in the world? But if we have a handle on what is happening within us, then working with, exploring and understanding these categories can help us a lot. Equanimity is a heightened awareness of our own discrimination faculties – with compassion for ourselves and others. It's mindfulness's superhero friend.

Being immersed in the present moment is not a quick fix. Developing an equanimity mindset is a lifelong process, but you can start now.

Developing an Understanding of Equanimity

A clearer understanding of equanimity can help anyone to develop the attribute of non-judgement taught in mindfulness and experienced during meditation. In practice, evaluating any barriers to equanimity can enable people to map out and try to overcome potential obstacles, which may subsequently improve the therapeutic process.

A fundamental lesson that equanimity teaches us is that it is not our experiences that take us out of kilter and overwhelm us, but our attachments and aversions to those events. Therefore, it makes sense to explore and understand further why we think the way we do. The first thing we need to do to develop our understanding of equanimity is to distinguish it from 'non-judgement' and 'de-centering'. However, these mindful skills do play pivotal roles in contemporary mindfulness research and western psychology, so it is important to understand the fundamental differences between these skills and equanimity.

Non-judgement

Non-judgement is the ability to accept an experience that gives rise to some form of discomfort within us, such as frustration, anger, fear or disgust. Non-judgement clearly shares aspects of outer equanimity in that it is characterised by acceptance and patience towards others. However, there is little focus on compassion towards the self and/or others. And non-judgement can imply that an individual partly 'covers up' their true feelings in a bid to appease another, which is unhelpful because it can lead to thought suppression, withdrawal and an impact on our own self-esteem. To train ourselves to be non-judgemental is potentially to ask ourselves to repress, deny or withdraw from our own inner responses. Or we think, 'I know I shouldn't judge, but I do. I'll just act like I'm not judging in order to be perceived as a good person!' We have to be aware of this response in order to work with it.

With inner equanimity, on the other hand, we pay respect to our own discrimination faculties with compassion. That could make all the difference in making a healthier non-judgement.

Realising that there is an element within each of us, no matter how subtle, that is, to some extent, judging each and every situation is an important first step in understanding equanimity. While we may not be passing harsh and rigid judgements, we may well be evaluating what we like, dislike or feel indifferent about. Even when an individual perceives themselves to be non-judgemental, there is still a feeling of having an opinion, however mild, that with awareness an individual would recognise. This is the beginning of making unconscious bias conscious.

The non-reactivity aspect of equanimity implies a level of non-judgement, but it goes beyond this when considering our own discrimination faculties. That is, our own perceptions of 'like', 'dislike' and 'neutrality' are given brief attention or held in awareness before exercising non-judgement through a window of awareness towards oneself. There is an acceptance or acknowledgement of the role we are playing in relation to the object to be 'not-judged'. It is not enough to simply not judge the judgements; instead, aim to turn towards them with curiosity and an openness to learn from what they tell us.

Finally, non-judgement may imply compassion, but compassion may not be present. There is no requisite for compassion to even be considered when we think about non-judgement. Perhaps tolerance moves towards compassion, but tolerance is often a form of reluctant acceptance. Equanimity clearly brings into consideration compassion for the self and others, which goes well beyond non-judgement.

De-centering

De-centering is a skill present in mindfulness that helps us to observe our thoughts as events and not facts.[15] This implies that we observe our own feelings without identifying with them and listening to what they are trying to tell us. This again could result in thought repression or suppression if not adhered to correctly. De-centering closely relates to the non-reactivity aspect of mindful non-judgement and implies a level of insight towards oneself, and it is a valuable skill. However, this skill does not focus in on the tripartite elements of like, dislike or neutrality that are clearly present in equanimity. It is this information that could be useful and a valuable source of reflection. De-centering is linked even closer with equanimity than non-judgement, however, and it is distinct from some of the facets present in equanimity.

De-centering is critical when considering that we do not have to believe all our thoughts. But this needs refining with equanimity in that, although we do not have to believe all our thoughts, it is useful to understand the role our mind plays in projecting our feelings onto the thought. We will either like, dislike or find the thought neutral. In formulating this insight, we are then perhaps more readily able to overcome or disengage from our thoughts because we have accepted the role our mind is playing with them – perhaps even establishing why the thought may be present in the first place. Typically, our mind craves pleasurable thoughts, but it often finds itself inundated with negative thoughts.[16] This insight into the nature of our thoughts is perhaps useful in an emotionally regulative capacity.

---

15 Wells, A. (2005) Detached mindfulness in cognitive therapy: A metacognitive analysis and ten techniques. *Journal of Rational-Emotive and Cognitive-Behavioural Therapy*, 23, 337–355.

16 Rozin, P. and Royzman, E.B. (2001) Negativity bias, negativity dominance, and contagion. *Personality and Social Psychology Review*, 5(4), 296–320.

Extending Your Introspective Toolkit with Equanimity

Non-judgement and de-centering are well established for good reason and will continue to be useful in mindfulness and mindfulness research for years to come. However, it seems apparent that in a therapeutic capacity, equanimity – that also considers our unique discrimination faculties and has a role for self-compassion and compassion for others – has more to offer.

From a research perspective, if we do not fully understand equanimity, then we might ask study participants to accept all phenomenon without discernment (that is, without insight). This is not necessarily a good thing if you think about people's internal moral compasses and allegiances to ethics. For example, if someone commits a crime, there will be a level of discernment no matter how much we try to accept what has happened. So, with equanimity and full awareness (because the sense of self is not overly attached or averse to the discernment), we are able to accept things more easily with a sense of patience and fluidity. There is a certain wisdom that comes with acceptance. Being human involves discernment and judgement, so it is best to embrace this with equanimity so that we do not become overly emotionally involved with the object of our judgement. Equanimity acts as protection from over-emotional involvement. It is not judgement that is wrong per se; it is the self-attachment to the identified constructs of good, bad and neutral that embed the individual within a specific context and risk the potential for distortion.

The real beauty of equanimity lies in the contemplative nature of testing experience first-hand. It is not sufficient to simply hold a theory of mindfulness and claim to possess its treasure. We must embark on a journey into changing the way we relate to the world based on an experiential, heartfelt rawness of what it is to be human and what it truly means to live in the moment. But disharmony, frustration and unhappiness will still be present unless we work with our selves and temper those flames to protect ourselves.

It is our sense of self that passes the judgements of like, dislike and neutrality, and that has built up such rigid cognitive boundaries. An objective analysis of who we are in relation to the world enables us to expand attentiveness, but also requires meditation and the wisdom of equanimity. Without meditation (explored in Chapter 6) and equanimity, mindfulness may merely contribute to an intellectual exercise that we show or act out in the world, rather than the inner sense of peace and the experience of uprooting unwholesome habits that can be gained from equanimity. In other words, mindfulness may become an unregulated exercise that superficially tends to our concept of wellbeing and may serve only as a refreshing interlude in an otherwise distracted, movie-like existence.

Basic mindfulness techniques like the body scan and mindful breathing teach us to observe and separate experience from judgement. It is identifying self with experience that leads to judgement. This then generates the ability to become present within our experience and cultivates our ability to monitor our own sense of attachment, aversion and clinging, to instead focus on non-reactivity and acceptance.

Equanimity is further developed when we embark on an inner monitoring process of the various thoughts and emotions that arise on a moment-to-moment basis. As we home in on the present moment, we are able to deactivate how we adversely label, so we can monitor and respond rather than react. The net of identification is less able to capture and instead we have an opportunity to open up with curiosity to the present-moment experience as it occurs. The ability to monitor the content of our minds and open up to the fleeting nature of thoughts enables us to observe how all content passes and only lingers as we begin to identify with like or dislike, attachment or aversion. This enables a more peaceful and contented mind that is able to observe the transitory movement of experience.[17]

One of the only definitions of equanimity found in the scientific literature defines it as "the suspension of judging experience to be intrinsically good or bad".[18] This suggests that equanimity refines the mental discernment associated with judgement, which is not fully captured via current mindfulness definitions. Modern-day mindfulness incorporates attention, awareness and non-judgemental curiosity, yet it appears that equanimity (taught as a separate construct in Buddhism in order to develop compassion) has been overlooked. A key question looms: how important is equanimity in mediating the emotional regulatory

17 Feldman, C. and Kuyken, W. (2019) *Mindfulness: Ancient Wisdom Meets Modern Psychology*, Guilford Press.
18 Farb, N.A., Anderson, A.K. and Segal, Z.V. (2012) The mindful brain and emotion regulation in mood disorders. *Canadian Journal of Psychiatry*, 57(2), 70–7.

affect in modern-day mindfulness? And, if it is important, how do we know what to measure and by what instrument? Perhaps the proposed definitions of equanimity that I shared at the beginning of this chapter (which include non-reactivity, self-compassion, compassion for others and awareness of discrimination) can create a path towards working with the concept of equanimity within modern-day mindfulness.

In responding to our own mind's reactivity with equanimity, we grow our ability to extend this outward to all our relationships and beyond. Jon Kabat-Zinn advocates that mindfulness without 'kindfulness' or 'heartfulness' is not mindfulness, implying that the roots of mindfulness go beyond the self to developing care for others. At present, mindfulness is a potent tool for stress reduction and for building acceptance and resilience towards experience, as well as providing therapeutic benefits. However, it perhaps falls short of capturing some of the fullest qualities of equanimity, such as developing self-compassion and compassion towards others.

To ensure that when we practise mindfulness we do not slide into mediocrity (a form of indifference given its emphasis on non-reactivity), or, at worst, psychological dissociation (which is a way of disconnecting from our own thoughts, feelings, memories and sense of identity), I suggest some attitudes here that capture the spirit of equanimity. This is really important because without closer inspection you could brand equanimity as a form of simple apathy or disconnection, which is very much not the case. Instead, it is as if our inner experience is that of a balloon on a string. When things happen, we let go of the balloon so it gently rises, but we do not lose sight of it because we are still connected by holding on to the string! We are just able to observe the feelings come and go and recognise why they are present.

The following attitudes encapsulate the spirit of equanimity:

> Monitoring our own discernment towards experience/feelings and patiently withholding from reaction.
> Being aware of our own mental discernment.
> Remaining calm in times of conflict.
> Staying even-tempered towards all people (and, when helping others, not becoming attached or being too indifferent).
> Expanding tranquillity and even-mindedness towards happiness and unhappiness, pleasure and pain.

> Lessening the sense of attachment, repulsion and indifference towards others.
> Extending the parameters of compassion towards those we like, and also to those we dislike.
> Remaining steadfast, open and present in our interactions in daily life without wishing for anything to be different.[19]

This list is significant in driving home the message of overall balance that can be accomplished with equanimity: that we can identify with things, but not in an over-the-top way; we can feel things to the maximum, yet not be consumed by them. We are able to create a buffer from our subjective experience without reaction, but not becoming robotic! We can still very much live a full, emotional life, just with more mental protection.

Addressing Some Common Misconceptions about Equanimity

Equanimity has been my professional focus for five years now. During this time, I have encountered some interesting questions about the nature of equanimity. The following questions may help put some common misconceptions to bed as you develop a greater understanding of equanimity.

Equanimity is too hard to practise because it requires a direct retraining of our brains, which naturally gravitate towards pleasure and try to avoid conflict. Retraining our brains would be a contradiction of what it means to be human. We are creatures of habit: we enjoy what we like and avoid what we don't like. However, neuroscience has proved that we can become better and wiser in relation to our impulses. Our overarching survival mode, often referred to as 'fight or flight', works on primitive instinct (whether to defend ourselves or flee from a predator) rather than logic, and supersedes other brain activity in certain situations such as conflict. We understand now why part of our brains are like that, but we don't necessarily have to act in survival mode – unless you need to run away from a tiger in the jungle! In everyday life, when the only drama is usually the self-created narrative of our own thoughts, we certainly shouldn't be held to account by

19 Weber, J. (2019) Operationalising equanimity in clinical practice: A mindful approach. Clinical Psychology Forum, October 2019.

our primitive responses. We can observe our fight-or-flight responses with equanimity and, if unnecessary, not act on them. So yes, we are creatures of habit, but it is we who have set the parameters of our own reality.

When we are working with equanimity, we directly shift the ways in which we consciously relate to the world. We make wise choices for our actions rather than acting from impulse. Over time, this will change the structure of our brains because we can create healthy thought patterns, and a system of wise responses. Our brains have enormous capacity for adaptation and change. Then, being equanimous perhaps becomes easier over time and we expand the parameters of our own compassion because an equanimous response will come more naturally.

Equanimity seems to be very robotic – if we shouldn't get over-attached, does this mean we have to reduce our emotions: allow a little joy, but not too much? That sounds quite debilitating.

There are two great enemies of equanimity. The first is indifference, or apathy. This is often called the *near enemy* in Buddhism: the quality of being so dissociated with life that we just do not care anymore. No matter what happens, we just experience life as if we are not part of it; a mere passive witness to an ever-wild ride. However, this is not the quality I wish to promote here. This state of being sounds incredibly unhuman. We are emotional beings. Equanimity does not say, 'Whoah, hold on there, you are responding and being emotional and that is a bad thing.' It is more like imagining a quality controller observing the action, monitoring why they think a particular response is the best one, where it has come from, and has given it the all-clear from a quality and compassionate perspective. To put it simply, there is insight into what we are doing. So by all means, we can yell in the streets with glee when we are happy and cry our eyes out when we are sad. Equanimity is wisdom, and over time this translates to a different experience with reality. It should not, by any means, suggest that we cut ourselves off from life because we 'see through it' or we just don't care.

The second enemy of equanimity is over-identification and attachment – the opposite of indifference. This is often cited as the *far enemy* in Buddhism: being overly attached to things. We run the risk of exaggerating the qualities of certain objects in our minds (this could be anything from our partner, car, house, job or favourite sandwich!) and then seeking those objects as a source of happiness. And for sure – we should enjoy them! However, we should not over-exaggerate them and rely on them to make us happy. With the understanding that all things are subject to change and are transient moments in time, it would be a mistake to project a sense of permanence onto these objects. For example, the sandwich will get stale, our partner might turn out to be incompatible or the car might become rusty! At the same time, I'm not suggesting we should stay away from the things that give us pleasure, but equanimity gives us some insight into our thoughts in relation to the pleasurable item. If we over-identify or become over-attached (or even infatuated!) to someone or something, we may experience many highs in life – but unless this remains constant (which it will clearly not), then we will eventually be left feeling dissatisfied, frustrated and angry. This is why infatuation as a teenager is so tantalising: we experience highs we could never reach again, but may spend the rest of our lives trying to replicate.

So there is a balance to strike, somewhere in the middle, between indifference and over-identification. We do not become robotic with equanimity – we are still going to experience the highs, lows and in-betweens of life – but we won't get pulled in all directions from the storm. Importantly, equanimity does not ask you to stop being you. It encourages you to become a wiser version of you.

It sounds like I will spend too much time second-guessing what is happening inside my head, which might make me more cautious and affect my personality. Might thinking like this slow me down?
I get where this question is coming from, because with equanimity there needs to be an awareness that oversees what is happening before you act. We need to monitor how we are thinking and ensure we modify our behaviour in order to be equanimous. I understand if this come across as clunky – like living in self-analysis!

We need to separate equanimity into parts. We develop *insight* over time to appreciate equanimity in its purest form. Then there is the *experiential* component that we develop as part of this insight, but also through meditation and more direct personal experience. This then creates a new strain of equanimity in our minds so, over time, it becomes a more natural response.

A magnet analogy may help here. When one magnet attracts another, it moves towards the other magnet with a powerful compulsion. With equanimity, we reverse the poles; we gently withhold the compulsion with insight. With the poles reversed, there is a softness, a barrier, a space in which anything is possible. This, for me, is symbolic of equanimity.

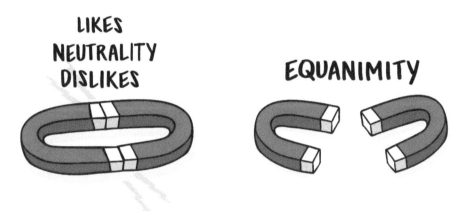

Equanimity does not jar. There is just this soft, subtle space that emerges between thought and action. This doesn't slow us down but becomes more natural over time, rather than feeling like a process of awkward actions.

Where is the reward for us? When we do things we like, we receive pleasure, but with equanimity it is as if we are cutting off this experience.
Think about what we understand as 'reward'. Do we mean we are replacing what gives us pleasure with equanimity? Because equanimity does not replace pleasure. It, of course, has a place for it, but as a wise form of pleasure. Therefore, we enjoy what we enjoy but not in an over-the-top way that means we suffer when it stops. We don't enjoy things at the expense of others or in a way that is detrimental to ourselves. Being equanimous means we fully experience being ourselves. We may stop doing things simply to please or impress others, or to play into any social role. Because we become more in tune with our own sense of self, we act more authentically. In this way, we begin a therapeutic relationship with ourselves, nurturing ourselves to be the best versions of ourselves we can be. We might also find things we do not necessarily like: why we react in certain ways, why we think the way we do. We learn to understand our

own habits, so we can break free from them if we wish to do so without judgement or self-loathing.

Takeaway Points:

> Equanimity runs deeper than non-judgement and de-centering.
> Developing our understanding of equanimity relies on extending our understanding of the key attitudes of equanimity.
> Like all new things, there are misconceptions about equanimity – we shouldn't allow misconceptions to pollute our understanding.

Chapter 3: Understanding Your Sense of Self: Who Am I?

Science is a means of analysing and describing the world that does not depend on any philosophical world view. But science has its limitations. While analysis of biodiversity, climate change and DNA are undoubtedly fantastic and essential pursuits, science cannot explain how consciousness arose or what happens when we die, so the more profound questions of life remain unanswered: 'Why am I here?' 'Where will I go when I die?' 'What about ethics, altruism and transcendence?'

In critiquing mindfulness, we are beginning to ascertain the value of equanimity to our experience and understanding of life in a way that goes beyond what science can explain. This chapter explores an additional and essential component that should be understood alongside mindfulness and equanimity: our sense of self, and how we can show compassion to ourselves and others, through exploring meaning and purpose.

Compassion for Ourselves and Others

Unless we wish to dwell in a constant state of conflict, we need the ability to understand someone else's situation. We also need to have the desire to change our own situation if we wish to become better versions of ourselves and increase our own wellbeing. We are all born with compassion, but this needs to be nurtured and encouraged rather than assuming that what we are born with is enough. Compassion is not a finite resource and can expand if we wish. In order to understand our own levels of compassion, we need to give a little analysis to who we are. Or, at least, who we think we are! But, before we go out and try to be compassionate to everyone in the world, we would also greatly benefit from self-compassion. This is because we are better able to take care of others if we have first taken care of ourselves. The airline instruction of first putting on your own oxygen mask before helping anyone else is a perfect analogy here. All religious faiths – their codes of conduct, verses on ethics and spiritual leaders – spread the message of compassion. From a purely logical reasoning, it certainly seems like a fundamental antidote to the divisiveness and conflict that ensues in the 21st century. In order for us to work with self-compassion, and then compassion for others, we need to work with our own cognitive rigidity – that is, who we think we are – and take on a little introspection. Without this, we are basically just limited by our own thinking. Without loosening and opening the way we think and lowering the walls of the good, the bad and the neutral, we may only be able to be compassionate within those parameters. How can we find the balance between caring for ourselves (self-compassion) and caring for others (compassion)? This balance is needed because otherwise we might find ourselves reaching burnout or compassion fatigue if our compassion for others is unskilful and overlooks ourselves. Or it may mean we ignore the plight of others because our own unfulfilled needs get in the way of trying to help. We could even become overly self-indulgent, yet never seem to feel fulfilled.

We are able to give blood because we can replace what we lose due to the miracle of our bodies. Compassion, too, is not a finite resource. We only experience difficulties such as compassion fatigue or burnout if we hold an incorrect view or attitude towards compassion.

Many people feel a sense of burnout or apathy, as if they have squeezed out the last drop of their compassion. Recognising and learning when we feel stretched or drained is an act of self-compassion. Giving ourselves the space or tools to recuperate is an act of self-compassion. Then, getting back into the dirt is an act of self-compassion as well as an act of compassion towards others. There is a continual and fluid exchange between moments. There are no blockages, hard feelings or obstacles to compassion. This is just a simple balancing act. Awareness of how the mind continually changes, observes, interacts and judges is us balancing on the tightrope. We are standing on a tightrope, walking step by step. It is only through non-awareness and distraction that we are likely to fall off.

Nurses, social workers and teachers often experience the phenomenon of compassion fatigue. We need to take responsibility for the lack of mental protection we often afford ourselves during the process of giving, helping or providing empathy. By mental protection I mean a loving awareness towards ourselves and others in the moment, and adopting an attitude of equanimity that buffers us from overly emotive or involved responses.

Self-compassion has entered the mainstream research paradigms.[20] One recent study looked at 1,700 doctors, nurses and medical students

20 Neff, K.D. (2012) The science of self-compassion. In: C.K. Germer and R.D. Siegel (Eds.), *Wisdom and Compassion in Psychotherapy: Deepening Mindfulness in Clinical Practice* (pp. 79–92), Guilford Press.

and reported how self-compassion moderated the relationship between stress and burnout.[21] I believe there is a need to focus on how we teach mindfulness and self-compassion in the classroom, especially to those in caring professions, and then how this transcends into teaching compassion itself.

Trying to teach these qualities that are subjective, experiential and tacit in comparison to more logical and academic content is tricky. Many of my fellow teaching colleagues have cited the dilemma of standing up in front of people and lecturing on qualities such as compassion and feeling rather demotivated. There is a need to not only offer theoretical components in relation to these virtuous qualities, but also experiential encounters.

Mindfulness is not only an idea but also a practical tool that a person must self-navigate. So too, must meditation, self-compassion, compassion and equanimity be tasted as well as taught.

Unpicking Our Sense of Self – Judgements and Desires

In public health studies there are some famous models of behaviour change that can help us to understand who we are.[22] For example, in health behaviour, a great deal of attention is given towards an individual's attitudes, drives, beliefs and values. Society helps to shape our values, and we carry with us our own drives for sex, pleasure and so forth. This all culminates in a sense of self that may hold strong, fixed judgements towards itself and the world (I talk more about judgements in Chapter 4). As we begin our journey with mindfulness, we begin to relax and loosen our judgements. The wisdom of equanimity that is present during this process stops it from being a selfish pursuit. Unless we work with our sense of self, we run the risk of honing our mindfulness without developing compassion.

If we objectively examine who we are and take into account all the different factors that have helped mould our sense of self (gender, age, ethnicity and so on) then we can learn who we are and why we think the way we do. We can go on and on considering our different influences

21 Dev, V., Fernando, A.T. and Consedine, N.S. (2020) Self-compassion as a stress moderator: A cross-sectional study of 1700 doctors, nurses, and medical students. *Mindfulness*, 11, 1170–1181. https://doi.org/10.1007/s12671-020-01325-6.
22 Becker, M (1974) The Health Belief Model and personal health behavior. *Health Education Monographs*, 2, 324–473.

(including our earliest friends' tastes and our classroom teachers). Then, once we begin mindfulness practice, we start to observe these factors from a greater distance. This generates wisdom and understanding about how likely we are to judge others. We experience an investigative disentangling of ourselves. We learn that this conditioning does not necessarily have to define us, and how and why we judge the way we do does not have to be so rigid.

The concoction of our own psychological makeup and demographic variables squeezes our identity and our responses into tiny compartmentalised judges (the wig and gown type you see on television dramas), who regularly and indiscriminately lay sentence upon ourselves and others. The judges form a strong part of our identity that runs the show. The trouble is, we are all bound to our tiny geographical courtrooms, and they're often invisible. The judgements come from our minds and we don't always realise that we're making them. Based on our identity and makeup, we routinely carry out categorisations that give rise to strict judgements and sentencing of events and experiences to the prison cells of good, bad and neutral. Our judgements are barriers to equanimity and are of significant importance. Without understanding these barriers, we restrict our potential.

This Wu Wei proverb provides a paradox of action and non-action (Wu Wei – meaning 'non-doing' – is from Taoism) and is attributed to the famous philosopher Lao Tzu: "Mind flows like water, reflects like a mirror and responds like an echo."[23]

The proverb is immediately soothing to read, sounds wonderful and sums up what, in essence, equanimity promotes. However, in reality, the water of our mind often comes up against dams in the river – barriers to equanimity.

The dams, representing judgements of good, bad and neutral, clog up the agility of the water, which reacts as it hits the dams, causing a build-up rather than gently passing along its journey. Certainly too, we have a problem with the mind being like a mirror if we hold on to hard and fast judgements about the world rather than simply reflecting them away. Finally, the concept of the mind like an echo signifies a fluidity or looseness that permits a form of clarity in what it sees: it does not react immediately, but learns to respond with wisdom, softly, like an

23 Gregory, J. (2018) *Effortless Living: Wu-Wei and the Spontaneous State of Natural Harmony*, Inner Traditions.

echo. Combined, we see the nature of our discriminating mind causes anything but peace and buoyancy, but rather drags us along and turns many streams into white water rapids. To say we are up against it is an understatement. Let us grab onto the raft of equanimity to keep us afloat.

Do we even know what the mind wants and for what purpose? This comes back to awareness – a mindful mind, flowing like water, may be conscious of how it evaluates reality and checks up on whether the motive to act is for selfish or compassionate reasons. But, in reality, we often do not have enough mental space or conscious awareness of our day-to-day wants, needs and judgements. We often just live on autopilot, trying to have more of the nice stuff in life: engaging in pleasant conversations, eating delicious food, having sex, drinking, or feeling a sense of warm camaraderie at work or in the community.

This is pretty much how we measure whether we have had a 'good' day. How well did we get what we wanted? If we sense that we had more of the good stuff than the bad, then we can sign the day off as a good day, and vice versa. But reality isn't as straightforward. We often have mixed experiences and sometimes cannot distinguish what was good or not. Was it a good thing that we had a delicious three-course meal out, or was it overindulgent and harmful to our health and bank balance? Do we then just cross that off as a neutral experience, or carry guilt about it?

We may quickly become overwhelmed by experiences based on these rigid ideas of good, bad, right and wrong. Yet underneath it all may lie the lesson. What were the motivations behind what we did? Were they altruistic or for personal gain? Here lies the inner conundrum. We may be inner hedonists for our own desires, but some may place sharing the good stuff on more of a pedestal. Some of us may say, 'I have done nothing but put others before me and now I am done,' in times of extreme tension. There is a dance going on between altruism and selfish pursuit. Either way, unless we analyse the self, how will we understand which one is winning?

Can we ever conduct a completely selfless act? This is an interesting and highly complex question. Perhaps some Buddhists spend their lives trying to do good things only to enhance their karmic merit banks. Would this deem their lives selfish? Deep down, only we know our motives and even then we can get caught up in doing the right thing via wrong reasoning. This is important to consider because each of us has individual nuances in relation to ideas of happiness, transformation and spirituality.

Pre-understanding and pre-cognition: the eye links to a discriminative undertone of whether this is a good, bad or neutral experience; whether it causes us aversion or is pleasing to our senses. As soon as an object is in awareness, a dynamic process has begun. There is a moment, so tiny, so minute, so subtle, so naked and raw that we almost never even notice it. Such is our panicked disposition to label and discern what exactly it is we are staring at. This overlooked embrace is swiftly engulfed by our very own discriminating mind. Whether we like, dislike, find pleasure or displeasure, find it wholesome or unwholesome, good or bad – the list goes on. We are seeking some reassurance that we understand and cognitively know what it is we have come into contact with. Safely categorising the moment into one of three domains (like, dislike, neutral), we can then interact with the object or experience on the basis of this understanding. Of course, this then readily gives way to stronger feelings, thoughts and subsequent behaviour. If we like the book then we carry on reading; if we dislike it, we discard it.

But where do these basic (at first glance), primitive drives come from? And they are not wrong, right? We need to discern to make choices, plan, analyse, conclude and function in everyday society with our families, friends and other relationships. Are they what make us unique? These drives are the reason you think you are unique.

To explore this further, in the next chapter I delve deeper into our individual 'judgement blueprint' – the spectrum across which we make judgements about the world around us.

Takeaway Points:

> Caring for ourselves as well as others can help us to have a deeper understanding of who we are – and to be aware of the risks of burnout and compassion fatigue. You cannot pour from an empty cup!
> There is a dance going on inside us between altruism and selfishness, and we need to be able to analyse and understand ourselves to better evaluate our true motivations – and therefore know whether altruism or selfishness is winning.
> We may not appear to be who we think we are. At least question that!

Chapter 4: A Continuum of Judgements

Before working with the skill of non-judgement, judgement may be better understood by thinking about a *continuum* or *scale* of judgement.

Less judgemental   More judgemental

Within the continuum, we have four domains that create our own unique and individual judgement 'blueprint'.

Figure 4.1: The four domains.

These domains create a construction of self and give us insight into how we are affected both personally and socially. We have been uniquely constructed by both what we entered the world with and the social world we came into. In this chapter, I explain how these four domains (innate, social, interactive and reflective) can create barriers that get in the way of our ability to be equanimous.

Introducing the Continuum of Judgements: The Four Domains

The four domains of judgement cause barriers to equanimity because each of them creates the circumstance for how and why we judge. These then act as potential barriers because equanimity is about being non-reactive and having compassion towards our own judgemental mind.

Our quick-fire, discriminative mind states (of like, dislike and neutral) act like a gangster in a shoot-out. We see, we judge; we hear, we judge; we think, we judge. Bang! Bang! Bang! – but the only casualty is our sense of self because we continually label and project onto objects and seek to validate our sense of identity. We're shooting at ourselves, yet moving on wounded to the next victim, not realising it's ourself again. It's amazing how many shots we can fire, yet we still feel energised to carry on. In fact, these wounds don't kill us; they just reinforce who we think we are and bolster our old thinking patterns. That's the real killer. We become more and more fixed into who we think we are based on these judgements. Shooting around with the bullets ricocheting back to us, trapping us in a prison with only three walls – the good, the bad and the neutral. There's a new film here, I'm sure!

With equanimity, we aim for mental calmness. This is not to say that mental calmness always contains the absence of judgements, although that would be nice. It comes from the idea that we do not define ourselves by these judgements. Our likes and dislikes should not hold so much sway over us; they are merely a way in which we have grown to habitually relate to the world, but they do not have to define us. Without equanimity, we live our lives through these categories as if they rule and our autonomy is a secondary guest. Our free will plays second fiddle as a passive witness to the almighty judgement continuum. We become disheartened by not getting what we want, and overexcited by getting a little bit of what we do want, only to see it all change hour after hour. It's like a constant battle with these categories, the war commanders. If only we could see that if we lower the gun, the commanders only want the victory for themselves and victory is never enough.

Essentially, judgements *can* be observed without reaction, and greater insight into our barriers to equanimity (explored in Chapter 5) can help us realise that we have a tendency to be set in our ways and that it is difficult to constantly satisfy the demand for pleasurable things. So we enter a hamster-wheel-like existence, on a hedonic treadmill, judging things because we think it will help us satisfy our inner discontent, yet it only seeks to serve more judgements.

Figure 4.2: The four domains of judgement contribute to our sense of self.

Each time we judge, we create an idea that we then respond to and interact with. What we are ultimately judging is who we are through the lens of our own sense of self, illustrated in Figure 4.2. This is sounding rather complicated, so let's break it down into the four domains in the continuum of judgements model (innate, social, interactive and reflective) to give a clearer picture of how these types of judgements can act as barriers to equanimity.[24]

1. Innate judgements

The 'innate' level of judgement refers to what we come into the world with; our genetically predetermined basic instincts of like, dislike and neutrality. These base notes determine how we relate to and interact with the world – you could say they are our primordial layers of judgement that

24 Weber, J. (2017) Mindfulness is not enough: Why equanimity holds the key to compassion. *Mindfulness & Compassion*, 2(2), 149–158.

begin via the gene–environmental interaction, manifesting as conscious or unconscious judgements about the world around us.[25] In other words, a newborn child has an innate sense of judgement towards things depending on their physiological functioning. These primordial feelings of like, dislike and neutrality give rise to solidified judgements and represent the 'nature' side of the nature–nurture debate; that is, what we come into the world with and why we are all unique. Even babies prefer individuals who share their tastes, compared to those with contrasting views.[26] On a purely observational level, this is evident in young children displaying preferences for things, people, attachment figures, emotions and memories.[27]

The nature–nurture debate has always been a source of interesting dialogue. Famous pioneers such as Charles Darwin (famous for the theory of evolution and 'survival of the fittest') and Sigmund Freud (the founder of psychoanalysis) both argued that humans have an inbuilt capacity for emotional expression, with instinctual drives and a pre-set biological nature.[28] If a person identifies intensely with their inherent views (such as what they find attractive), then their sense of self is closely attuned to their feelings and so they communicate their judgements from an innate level.

The innate domain is the 'inner you'. The Christopher Nolan film *Inception* does a great job of exploring the way that our dreams take on different layers. The film gradually reveals elements of who we are by hiding our deeper thoughts and desires further down the layers.[29] In relation to us here right now, the 'us' that is raw, without makeup or storyline, the primal sense of self, drives our instinctual behaviour forward. Our innate animalistic likes and dislikes relate to instinct and a deep sense of what we find attractive, unattractive or neutral based on our nature. We are all unique judgement-givers because of our inherent biological and nature-given endowments.

25 Kandel, E. (2013) The new science of mind and the future of knowledge. *Neuron*, 80(3), 546–560.

26 Wynn, K. (2016) Origins of value conflict: Babies do not agree to disagree. *Trends in Cognitive Sciences*, 20, 3–5.

27 Tasimi, A. and Johnson, M.K. (2019) Children's initial responses and beyond: Effects of niceness and similarity on preference, giving, and memory, *Child Development*, 90(2), 432–440.

28 Ritvo, L. (1992) *Darwin's Influence on Freud: A Tale of Two Sciences*, Yale University Press.

29 Nolan, C. (2010) *Inception*, Warner Bros. Pictures.

Geneticists may provide us with reams of technical information about our DNA, and religious followers may exclaim that our innate judgements come from above. But to engage with this innate domain is to have an open mind. We won't find a direct answer, but simply leave open an unexplainable question. There is something deep within us that is unique, unconscious and mysterious, and it is okay to have these questions about where our innate judgements come from unanswered.

2. Social judgements

The 'nurture' side of this debate is represented in the social domain; that is, we are 'conditioned' by role models in society. *Conditioning* relates to the process of accustoming a person to accept and behave certain ways in certain circumstances. From studies with geese (which follow humans in the absence of a recognised mother) and monkeys (baby monkeys prefer warm cloth 'mums' over wire ones with food),[30] developmental theories are now laden with ideas around why humans flourish or flop. Through conditioning, an individual moulds their behaviour, attitudes and beliefs. What is socially desirable as a social norm or expectation seeps into our collective consciousness.

The social world creates many opportunities for us to form judgements. Judgements are made by ourselves or are shaped and moulded by the social world. From an internal perspective, we live up to what society expects from us, which includes our parents/carers, family and peers. Social desirability determines how we strive to fit in, be seen as useful and find our place in the world. We categorise phenomenon in a way that shows us adapting to our surroundings and navigating through complex environments by judging things that help us flourish, which further strengthen our values, beliefs and attitudes.

Many social constructs influence us in our external judgements too. The education system, police, political figures, the media and civic institutions all leave imprints on us, which we then categorise into what we like, dislike and are not particularly bothered about. Think about how all of these aspects might influence our values, attitudes and beliefs on a daily basis.

Also consider how we behave in order to fit in. We only have to think back to our days in the school playground to see how we may have acted

---

30 Vicedo, M. (2010) The evolution of Harry Harlow: from the nature to the nurture of love. *History of Psychiatry*, 21(2), 190–205.

or behaved in a way seen to be socially acceptable in order to climb higher in the social standings. In this sense we bring our innate domain with us into the social realm. Society imposes upon us from the top down and we too shape our own feelings from the bottom up. A reciprocal dance of social judgement solidification takes place. We can begin to deepen our understanding of our judgements on the continuum by building from innate judgements to more social judgements. This is both true from the perspective of social psychology and Buddhist psychology when taking into account self and social conditioning.

This two-component view that contains both an inner and outer element of social conditioning ('inner' in terms of our own social desirability and 'outer' in terms of being moulded from the outside in) of how we accrue our feelings on a social level plays out a type of battle for assumed power. The innate and social judgements continually dance between distraction and awareness. It is here that our base level of innate judgements is intensified via the social world.

Here the individual conveys a set of internal social judgements that are either reinforced or challenged based on an individual's tendency towards making judgements. This can solidify innate judgements on a more unconscious level, yet can also be changed via the tenacity of experience and the personality in question. *External* social judgements relate to the multitude of possibilities that social institutions or agencies can manifest as conscious or unconscious influences upon a person. *Internal* social judgements refer to our inner reactions that seek approval and acceptance from the social world. These combined might impact behaviour, making people wary of each other or eliciting either positive or negative judgements about themselves or others. An example is someone holding strong beliefs about a group of people because of reading certain newspapers, or someone acting out to impress a group of people. This behaviour could even be detrimental. Once someone has gained approval for behaving a certain way, they may develop a strong belief that their actions were the best way, thus fabricating a deeply held judgement in relation to this behaviour. The risk of this could be that individuals suffering from low self-esteem, low confidence or non-awareness may formulate judgements based solely on the desire to fit in, such as a shy member of a group trying to impress a bully.

The risk of social manipulation is perhaps best demonstrated in the Cambridge Analytica (CA) scandal where Donald Trump hired CA to harvest about 87 million Facebook profiles. A 'dark post' feature on Facebook enabled personalised ads to reach targeted individuals, a strategy that is thought to have played a key role in President Trump's 2016 victory over Hillary Clinton. The scandal showed that we are vulnerable to psychological manipulation because the way people presented themselves through social media allowed them to be profiled due to social media targeting. CA managed to 'profile' individuals in order to manipulate personalised advertisements.[31] The notion of psychological vulnerability is perhaps best demonstrated in a recent study,[32] which found that computer personality predictions based on 'likes' were more accurate than that of the 86,220 participants' close friends.

3. Interactive judgements

An interactive judgement is one that we have during an interaction with someone. It relates to how we have a tendency to be distracted in moment-to-moment interactions. Think of a recent interaction with someone, and consider how quickly you were categorising the experience as good, bad, useful, unhelpful, fun or boring. Your judgement probably depends on how mindful you were at the time, and how much you were affected physically by your mood, how much you had eaten and slept, what the other person was wearing and so on. Most of the interactive judgements that we accumulate via our innate and social layers colour – and to a certain extent pre-determine – our present-moment experience. We spend a considerable amount of time 'within' the mind, rather than 'in' the present moment, and therefore we are often lost in dominant judgemental modes of being. Awareness of our own feelings, and how these may in turn influence our emotions and our behaviour with others, is a key facet of mindfulness-based therapy. Further, this relates to physical awareness because our mind and body are so closely related. Physical awareness means an awareness towards how our body relates to the moment – our posture, aches and pains and so on – and how this

31 Rehmen, I. (2019) Facebook-Cambridge Analytica data harvesting: What you need to know. *Library Philosophy and Practice*, [online], 2497.

32 Youyou, W., Kosinski, M. and Stillwell, D. (2015) Computer-based personality judgments are more accurate than those made by humans. *Proceedings of the National Academy of Sciences of the United States of America*, 112(4), 1036–1040.

may influence our mind in the moment. Positive and negative emotions, and how conscious we may be of them, also influence present-moment interactions.

4. Reflective judgements

The reflective judgement domain signifies that even after an experience, we categorise and theorise the experience as good, bad or neutral when we reflect on it. We relate our experience to the innate level, the social level and the interactive level of the present-moment experience to assign *meaning* to the experience. Without equanimity, however, this can counterintuitively stunt reflective progression and reinforce pre-existing maladaptive behaviours because we are always putting experiences into certain boxes that may feed anxiety, fears or stress. If an event happens that we categorise as bad, then we may replay it over and over in our minds which, in turn, may create anxiety. Post-event, the experience will be categorised on a conscious/unconscious level alongside previous layers of judgement, so the 'self' remains in a state of perceived control.

The reflective domain also considers how much memory influences our feelings. People reaffirm their core beliefs and sense of identity by remembering people/events in a certain way. This creates a barrier to equanimity because we end up relating to people based on our history with the person rather than taking them as they are in the moment. In a broader sense, the principle of 'cognitive consistency' refers to how an individual strives to hold all attitudes and beliefs in harmony.[33] Thus, in relation to memory, we reaffirm our core beliefs by memorising events, people and interactions in harmony with their individual narrative which, in the case of the model of judgement, would be a collection of the innate, social and interactive domains of judgement. For example, if I met a friend for lunch and conversation, I would likely categorise the experience afterwards as a positive one in my memory. Further, past memories are categorised in line with our sense of self, attitudes and beliefs. The four domains of judgement work in a reflexive manner, contributing to a whole sense of self in any given moment. However, the question is – are our domains healthy? Adaptive? Useful? Or are they flawed? Are we essentially making cognitively rigid judgements driven from a place of spontaneous subjectivity? How might our categorisations help or hinder us?

33 Festinger, L. (1957) *A Theory of Cognitive Dissonance*, Stanford University Press.

The Four Domains in Practice

It is especially helpful to see the judgement domains in practice because otherwise they remain lost in an intellectual abyss.

At this level you are very much acting from autopilot. You may have particularly strong views about things that feel almost incontestable. At your core, this innate sense of self acting automatically is linked with your brain's meta-cognitive core belief system. This may feel like whatever you experience at the felt level is taken very seriously. You *are* your feelings, as if there is almost no separation between your sense of self and the feeling. There just is. If you feel angry – you are anger. If you are jealous – you are jealousy. This, of course, is made even more compelling because of your habitual reactive tendencies that have built up over time. I'm not judging! There are literally thousands of synapses in your brain that have helped formulate a sense of self over time, so no wonder it takes six weeks of consistent behaviour change for you to experience any kind of real, more permanent change. Such is the power of habit. To help address the issue of innate judging, try asking these two questions: Where does this judgement come from? Why do I feel the way I do in comparison to others? Innate judging may be intertwined with a lot of fear; for example, if my feelings change, I will change. This is because we have put so much emphasis on who we think we are, and our sense of self is so wrapped up with our feelings that we actually perceive ourselves as our feelings rather than a transitory fleeting moment in time. Analyse whether a feeling is genuine by considering whether you find yourself being automatically irked by people or things, or find pleasure in praise and nice things, without noticing why.

These judgements are a little easier to analyse given that there are more tangible aspects of our social life that intertwine with a person. There can be little doubt that we are affected by social life and we also play up to it. This is highlighted by the split in the domain's internal and external sphere. Politics influences us because of the speed at which divisions become apparent. Rigid boundaries quickly appear around things with such real-world ideas. How do you feel when you read a newspaper headline that confirms what you thought? Or how easily is your stance on a topic influenced by your manager's views? Our external reactive judgements – influenced by politics, cultural norms, media, institutions, peers and loved ones – are all around us and inescapable, even if we're barely aware of their subtlety.

This layer allows us to play with all the things that serve to distract us, to throw us off balance or to keep us subdued. Our levels of distraction (hopefully lessened with our practice of mindfulness) mean we can momentarily pay attention to the unfolding of the judgement dance. Nevertheless, we must not underestimate the levels of neurosis that may occur due to present-moment distraction. This could be a mental image, a thought or something physical. Imagine we are in the moment, listening to a friend talk about something important, but our body is aching: we like the person we are talking to, and they are telling us something sensitive, but we cannot shake the feeling of discomfort. This then would affect the conversation, possibly meaning we try to rush through it.

This level relates to our categorisation post-interaction. Was it a good, bad or neutral experience? We put a label on an experience before, during and after it. Depending on how the nature of the action or conversation goes, our discriminative mind will be sure to quickly and effortlessly follow. Did the situation go your way or not? Here lies the direction of your discrimination. This also relates to the field of memory. How do your memories of a person interact with your present moment conversation with them? Do you change your words, alter your body language or think a certain way to adapt, accommodate or coerce?

The Inner Capitalist

The four domains on the continuum of judgement scale also present a model of 'self-fabrication', or creation. This points towards the idea of an 'inner capitalist' accumulating good things and shedding negative things. The term 'inner capitalist' applies to people who go out of their way to experience pleasure and avoid unpleasantness or pain. Given the four domains that make up our judgement tones, we are then likely to play out these judgements as a fixed and rigid reality. If we like something, we want to have it more and more. For example, we might want more chocolate. Why? Because of the simple reason that it will give rise to pleasure. If we dislike something, then we do not wish to be around it, or may even create a big aversion towards it. Why? Because of the simple reason that it will be experienced as unpleasurable. This is not just restricted to inanimate objects, but also people and relationships;

for example, if someone says something about us we do not like. In fact, these feelings will probably be stronger for people! Let's not forget the mid-ground: the feelings of neutrality. These are equally as important, as there is a tendency for mid-ground feelings of indifference to be ignored or drift into aversion, given that these objects or people will give rise to neither pleasure nor unpleasantness (explored more in Chapter 5).

As inner capitalists, we become greedy for pleasurable experiences and the things we like, and we keep anything we dislike at arm's length. This is seemingly harmless at first glance. But what happens when one person's likes clash with someone's dislikes? Or when both people seek the same source of happiness, but only one can have it, such as a promotion at work? Or when we only seem to experience feelings of dislike rather than pleasure, or vice versa? This is when barriers to mental wellbeing are created. When we exaggerate the good qualities of the things we perceive we like and seek those objects as the source of all happiness, this is what Buddhism refers to as attachment. Attachment is like a sticky sense of longing for an object or person and then, without the object, we are not happy and may become dissatisfied or mentally jaded. Over time, this can create a big problem! We may experience accumulative mental dissatisfaction and be close to feeling frustration, sadness or even depression. Thinking negatively can all too easily become our default position (self-sabotage).

Your World View

The four domains of judgement are perhaps best considered in relation to your world view. This is a controversial topic, but relevant if we want to genuinely engage with the spirit of equanimity. I was once asked during a session I was teaching, 'So, with equanimity, where do you get your reward?' This question really impacted me, as it showed that I had overlooked the short-termism of people's sense of gratification because of my own world view. For me, the idea that becoming a better version of yourself may not reap any benefits until the next life was solidly imprinted in my consciousness. That in itself meant I had not paid so much attention to teaching around the here-and-now benefits of equanimity.

Your own peace of mind positively affects those around you. This not only enables an equanimous person to be fully authentic as we engage in the moment with our real-life reactive mind, but also to be more present-focused and compassionate.

With a balanced mind and behaviour stemming from a place of wisdom, compassion towards the other person emerges. Even if the other person does not return to a sphere of mindfulness or equanimity, at least they are faced with a congruent communicator. Equanimity acts as quality control over our discriminating mind, an overseer checking the wisdom of our speech and actions. This is mindfulness's quality assurance. Our heightened awareness is able to monitor our subjective reactions and judgements and offer wise counsel. Of course, this may only be one-sided congruency (harmony or agreement), but if we can constructively align to another with an equanimous mind then at least we are giving the other person our authenticity. This is an act of grace, an act of love. What better way of working with people?

In reaping the reward of authenticity, we are also actively avoiding cognitive dissonance in terms of saying one thing and feeling another. This is common when we do something we wish we hadn't, then experience a deep sense of resentment. Or when we feel compelled to toe the socially acceptable line rather than behave how we really want to. This is how authenticity translates into peace of mind. Also, with the motivation of compassion, we can rest assured that we behaved in the best way possible, or at least tried to. So often does the dance of life require reflection and commitment to change. Embracing equanimity into the sphere of reflection propels us into self-examination. Our rewards become restraint, patience and virtuous action, which in turn enables us to transfer these onto others. Rewards then come back to us in the form of peace of mind and kindness from others. So, in actual fact, we need not wait for the next life nor should we have to embrace any particular world view to experience the purity and benefits of an equanimous mind.

The only world view we should start from is a compassionate one, which believes in self-development and is motivated with kindness and empathy for the self and others.

Takeaway Points:

> There are four judgement domains within us – innate, social, interactive and reflective – that act as barriers to equanimity. As a result of these domains, we have a strong and fixed sense of self, which determines our world view.

> Each of us is an 'inner capitalist'– we all seek pleasure and aim to avoid unpleasantness.
> Overcoming our barriers to equanimity can enable us to become more compassionate beings.

Chapter 5: Measuring Barriers to Equanimity

Many tools have been developed to measure mindfulness as a state of being, and its associated skills such as non-judgement. Often, a mixture of subscales focus on attention, awareness or non-judgement. However, at the time of writing, no tool has been developed to measure equanimity or the barriers to equanimity apart from my own, as far as I am aware.

Many well-designed psychometrics that measure mindfulness predominantly focus on interactive present-moment experience to do with attention and awareness. Some of the most well-used scales – namely the Kentucky Inventory of Mindfulness Skills (KIMS),[34] the Toronto Mindfulness Scale (TMS),[35] the Five Facet Mindfulness Questionnaire (FFMQ),[36] the Freiburg Mindfulness Inventory (FMI)[37] and the Philadelphia Mindfulness Scale (PHLMS)[38] – do not really delve into the arena of non-judgement. It is here that my tool for measuring barriers to equanimity – the Equanimity Barriers Scale[39] – steps into an arena of its own.

The scale is designed to tap into the reasons *why* individuals may face barriers to equanimity in relation to the four domains of judgement (innate, social, interactive and reflective – refer to Chapter 4 for more on these).

I identified 15 items that are statistically the strongest ways to measure the four domains from where we get our judgements.

---

34 Baer, R.A., Smith, G.T. and Allen, K.B. (2004) Assessment of mindfulness by self-report: The Kentucky Inventory of Mindfulness Skills. *Assessment*, 11(3), 191–206.

35 Lau, M.A., Bishop, S.R., Segal, Z.V., Buis, T., Anderson, N.D., Carlson, L., et al. (2006). The Toronto Mindfulness Scale: Development and validation. *Journal of Clinical Psychology*, 62(12), 1445–1467.

36 Baer, R.A., Smith, G.T., Lykins, E., Button, D., Krietemeyer, J., Sauer, S., Williams, J.M.G., et al (2008) Construct validity of the five facet mindfulness questionnaire in meditating and non meditating samples. *Assessment*, 15(3), 329–342.

37 Walach, H., Buchheld, N., Buttenmuller, V., Kleinknecht, N. and Schmidt, S. (2006) Measuring Mindfulness: The Freiburg Mindfulness Inventory (FMI). *Personality and Individual Differences*, 40(8), 1543–1555.

38 Zeng, X., Li, M., Zhang, B. and Liu, X. (2015) Revision of the Philadelphia Mindfulness Scale for measuring awareness and equanimity in Goenka's Vipassana meditation with Chinese Buddhists. *Journal of Religion and Health*, 54(2), 47–62.

39 Weber, J. and Lowe, M. (2018) Development and validation of the Equanimity Barriers Scale [EBS]. *Current Psychology*, 1–15. https://doi.org/10.1007/s12144-018-9969-5.

The Equanimity Barriers Scale

The following 15 sentences make up the Equanimity Barriers Scale. Each item is part of a subscale that correlates to one of the four judgement domains, as shown. Read each statement, then rate it on a scale of 1–7, where 1 is 'strongly disagree' and 7 is 'strongly agree'. (Please note that the word 'feelings' is used to simplify the terminology of 'like, dislike and neutral'.)

1. I am what I feel. (innate)
2. If my feelings change, then I will change. (innate)
3. My feelings towards others are influenced by my culture. (social)
4. The media influences my feelings towards others. (social)
5. Organisations or institutions influence the way I perceive others. (social)
6. My sense of self feels threatened by 'socially desirable' norms and expectations. (social)
7. Societal expectations influence the way I perceive my feelings. (social)
8. How I behave with others is influenced by my sense of physical wellbeing. (interactive)
9. When I know I should be feeling positive but actually feel negative, I feel a sense of tension. (interactive)
10. I sometimes wish I could control my feelings rather than be controlled by them. (interactive)
11. When someone says something I disagree with, I notice a sense of tension inside me. (interactive)
12. My behaviour with others is dependent on how I feel. (interactive)
13. All my actions are governed by emotions. (interactive)
14. My memories are strongly linked with my feelings. (reflective)
15. My memories influence how I interact with others. (reflective)

Now, add up your scores. Scoring the subscales separately will give you a better understanding of how to make sense of your own barriers to equanimity. If you prefer, go to www.equanamee.com to complete your assessment online.

Scoring			
The Innate subscale is out of 14. Scoring 7 or above is considered high, whereas scoring less than 7 is considered low.	The Social subscale is out of 35. Scoring 17 or above is considered high, whereas scoring less than 17 is considered low.	The Interactive subscale is out of 42. Scoring 21 or above is considered high, whereas scoring less than 21 is considered low.	The Reflective subscale is out of 14. Scoring 7 or above is considered high, whereas scoring less than 7 is considered low.

The 15 statements consist of four subscales. The first two items (1, 2) represent the *innate* aspect of self towards likes and dislikes.

If we score highly (7 or above) on the innate statements, we are so closely entwined with our innate sense of self and our likes, dislikes and neutralities that we relate to ourselves as our feelings and are likely to have high barriers to equanimity here. If we score highly on this domain then we are likely to have a very rigid sense of self (high cognitive rigidity at an innate level). You can spot an individual who has a strong sense of innate judgements because they will likely live their life as if their feelings are their only compass in which they navigate the world. They cannot be wrong, they are always right, and they perhaps blame or criticise others rather than spend any time in introspection. This should not be confused with passion, as this is often a positive trait. If you scored low on these questions then you might already have a sense of fluidity in the way you relate to the world in that your feelings do not necessarily define you and can be experienced as transient moments in time. You are aware of yourself to such an extent that you know that you are not always right.

The following five items (3, 4, 5, 6 and 7) represent the *social* domain of judgement. If we score highly (17 or above) on these, then we are likely to be greatly affected by the social world around us. This is negative if we have low awareness of this, as it suggests we may be open to social manipulation. Three items (3, 4 and 5) represent the effect of the social world upon us from external forces such as culture, media and organisations. Two of the items (6 and 7) represent social barriers stemming from the individual: what we do in relation to society that then acts as a barrier towards equanimity. These are the internal social judgements. In this case, the items focus on how much social expectation and norms influence us. Perhaps we are all likely to fall short on this subscale; however, increasing awareness of these factors is likely to act as a mediator in pushing back against the social world controlling us. It is important for us to have a high awareness in this domain because we need to be able to formulate our own opinions, not be easily swayed by media and social media, and protect ourselves from fake news. In a world of social media, this is an important domain in which we must develop awareness in order for a more equanimous mindset.

The next six items (8, 9, 10, 11, 12 and 13) represent the *interactive* domain of judgement. Here the items clearly link with physical wellbeing – for example, lack of sleep or a physical illness that makes people agitated or distressed (items 8 and 9). If we score highly on this domain (21 or above) then we are likely to be distracted in the moment. This domain also represents the ways in which the moment can feel disharmonious within us, such as item 11. Items 8, 9, 10 and 11 refer to inner harmony and items 12 and 13 are more behaviour based. Naturally, we require a level of awareness to do the noticing; however, these statements give a sense that, regardless of what happens to us externally, we continually bring our inner turmoil into the moment, either from our own side or from someone or something causing us disagreement. The interactive domain represents distraction from the 'now' due to these barriers to equanimity. Distraction is perhaps the opposite of mindfulness and, at its most extreme, can manifest as anxiety, depression or fear over time. A mind full of cognitive dissonance can contribute to stress and disharmony.

Finally, items 14 and 15 represent the *reflective* domain. This domain is characterised by the symbolic representation of memory and the idea that we judge others based on our previous associations with them. It also shows how we categorise interactions that leave us with a sense of whether that was a good, bad or neutral experience. If we score highly (7 or above) in this domain, then we may have a strong likelihood of categorising events and using memory to filter into present-moment interaction. The reflective domain shows us that, even out of a distracted interaction, we may still carry with us high barriers to equanimity with our memories that may take the form of clinging onto the past in the grip of nostalgia or rumination. If we score low on this subscale, then we may be more present-moment orientated and relate to the world in the present rather than in the grip of nostalgia.

Understanding the Score: The Real-world Implications of the Equanimity Barriers Scale

People who score highly on the scale have greater barriers to equanimity: they experience less self-compassion (because their inner critic has been let loose to dictate to them how they have done x, y and z wrong since they were born), and they have greater difficulty with regulating their emotions (because high barriers equate to an individual having such a rigid sense of self that they live and die through their sense of likes and dislikes and know nothing else). The scale sheds light on how different personalities may experience equanimity. For example, high barriers to equanimity correlate with increased anxiety, depression and difficulties in emotional regulation, because these traits relate to how a person reacts to themselves in varying contexts by catastrophising their experience. My research also showed that, with age, we tend to naturally lower our barriers to equanimity (maybe because we come to know ourselves better, the older we get). The less mindful we are, the more we relate to a fixed sense of self because we relate to our thoughts as if they are real, so we experience greater barriers to equanimity.

Fewer barriers to equanimity correlates with increased mental wellbeing, self-compassion and mindfulness. Fewer barriers to equanimity also seems to be correlated with personality traits such as conscientiousness and agreeableness. More specifically, the more mindful a person is, the fewer barriers to equanimity they face, which makes sense, given the implicit nature of equanimity being touched upon in regular mindfulness training. However, in terms of emotional regulation, people with greater barriers to equanimity are likely to deploy negative coping strategies in times of emotional distress, be more impulsive and have an attitude of non-acceptance, whereas lesser barriers to equanimity suggest a person is better able to emotionally regulate via enhanced awareness, strategic goal setting and sharper clarity.

In relation to self-compassion, those with greater barriers to equanimity will have harsher self-judgements, and more likelihood of self-isolation and over-identifying with experience, whereas those with lesser barriers to equanimity are likely to be more mindful and experience greater feelings of common humanity, which are both key facets of self-compassion. Those who report high generalised anxiety disorder and clinical depression have higher barriers to equanimity and those with lesser barriers have higher general mental wellbeing.

The Equanimity Barriers Scale provides an evaluation of the degree of our barriers to equanimity – or where we get our judgements from. It reveals how our sense of self can be related to others, and can be used as a framework to explore how and why we formulate our judgements. Understanding what drives our behaviour allows us to become more self-aware and behave in more helpful ways. Therefore, the scale is significant within the provinces of health and wellbeing, and is also important when taking into consideration working with others whom we perceive as difficult, or when working to resolve conflict.

We have identified our barriers to equanimity – the next step is overcoming those barriers to cultivate equanimity in daily life (Chapter 6).

Takeaway Points:

> Lower barriers to equanimity suggest increased mental wellbeing, the ability to be more mindful and a greater capability for self compassion.

> Higher barriers to equanimity suggest negative emotional regulation strategies, and an increased likelihood of experiencing generalised anxiety and depression.

> Personality traits and our age contribute to how we experience different barriers to equanimity. As we get older, we tend to experience fewer barriers (we get wiser!), while certain personality traits (such as neuroticism) suggest higher barriers to equanimity.

> The closer we relate to a fixed sense of self, the greater our barriers to equanimity, given our relationship with our own likes, dislikes and neutrality.

> If we can let go of our fixed sense of self and experience the moment as it is, we can live a more peaceful and fulfilling life!

Chapter 6: Cultivating Equanimity in Daily Life

So how do we begin *practising* equanimity? There are two aspects to this. The first is an 'intellectual' or 'wisdom' element. That is, the cognitive understanding of what it means to be equanimous: an understanding of how we might go about it. The second relates to meditation itself, which may be more familiar territory if you already practise mindful meditation.

The only way to really taste equanimity is to experience it first-hand. In this chapter, I share a short seven-step process that I hope you find useful for understanding equanimity more fully and enabling you to begin your journey. I then turn to how meditation can help you practise equanimity.

Seven Steps towards Greater Equanimity

In the following sections, I guide you through seven steps that can help you to understand and develop greater equanimity, using three examples showing what we might like, dislike or find neutral.

Step 1. Recognise Categorisation

Figure 6.1: Recognising categorisation.

We each have our own unique sponge-like minds that are ready to absorb our thoughts and feelings, which we categorise into what we like, dislike or find neutral: 'the conversation with my friend was interesting,' 'my memory of nearly drowning at the beach is scary,' 'the colour of her sweater is plain.' These may seem like trivial examples, but they are just to give a general impression of how we can put the seven steps into action. You will come up with better examples yourself!

Reflect upon your own internal categorisation. What do you experience either positively or negatively? What do you find neutral? Perhaps review your day today, the people in it, the conversations you had. What did you like, dislike or find neutral? This may take the form of an attitude, belief or value, or you may think of it more in practical terms. Where do you think these feelings come from?

Step 2. Identification Process

Figure 6.2: Identifying your experiences.

Once things enter our sponge-like minds, we begin to identify with them. We follow the trajectory of our perception (good, bad or neutral). Following the earlier examples: 'I liked what my friend said about me,' 'that memory was a scary one that I dislike,' 'I neither like or dislike the sweater, so it is neutral to me.'

We temporarily become lost in the thought or feeling and behave in relation to this felt experience.

Do you recognise when you are feeling these subtle undertones of like, dislike or neutral or do you only notice when you have become lost in the thought or an experience? Are you even conscious of how you may have categorised the experience?

Think now about how much these base tones of either like, dislike or neutrality modify your experiences in life. How strongly do they influence you? Instead, it is more helpful to identify them – to recognise that you are having these judgements – without identifying *with* them.

Step 3. Inner Equanimity Reacts

Figure 6.3: Equanimity responds to judgements. The figure represents a person mentally protected (by the umbrella), with an open heart of compassion.

Manifesting inner equanimity is hard, as it involves being very mindful. Being mindful of thoughts and events as transient, fleeting experiences rather than as a fixed and rigid reality enables us to see the bigger picture. This enables us to lessen our identification with the thought or experience as being intrinsically good or bad and to just observe the changing nature of whatever is presenting itself. All three of those internal experiences are transitory: one pleasurable (a nice chat with a friend), one not so pleasurable (a fearful memory) and one neutral (the plain sweater). We notice them all and understand why we feel that way towards them. This acts as mini wisdom towards our subjective experience!

For example, I can see that a thought has arisen and that my mind has given it a label of good, bad or indifferent because of my unique sponge-like mind. However, the thought is not me but a transient moment in time and not a fixed reality. Therefore, with self-compassion, I can let go of this thought without becoming over-identified with it. I am draining the thought or feeling of any potential to overly influence me. Thus, I remain in a light-hearted equanimous mood regardless of whatever thought or feeling comes next.

Rather than replay the scary beach scene over and over and give it a certain power to cause me anxiety, or go overboard with the conversation I had with my friend and now think I am a perfect person, I can embrace them as subjective experiences and be kind towards myself with them. I might think to myself, 'Poor me for experiencing the fear, but it was just a one off and I won't worry about future times swimming,' and 'It's nice to hear positive things for a change from my friends,' for example. Then I let the thoughts go so I can remain present in the moment. How likely are you to 'play out' the narrative in your head based on the projections of good/bad, right/wrong, wholesome/unwholesome? How likely does a thought or feeling lead to an emotive action or behaviour based on a strongly-held perception by your own discriminatory mind? Can you think of times in which you have reacted and then later regretted it? Instead of reacting with judgement, allow your inner equanimity to respond.

Step 4. Inner Equanimity Soothes

Figure 6.4: Equanimity can soothe your judging mind.

Do you notice your mind being biased towards good or bad experiences, towards people you like or dislike? Can you think of any experiences or people that you have judged based on your projection of likes/dislikes that you wished you had not?

Being open and accepting of all mental content regardless of whether we like, dislike or find the thought boring or neutral, enables us to create a harmonious, emotionally-regulative sponge-like mind that is not likely to suppress or deny thoughts or feelings, or over-identify with them. Inner equanimity enables us to observe our psychological makeup as it occurs in the moment (look at how the figure holds the categorisations in the palms of their hands) and give our fullest mindful attention to everything, regardless of the type of thought or experience. We do not suppress, repress or overindulge in thoughts because we are not our thinking. We are bigger than our thoughts, and this gives us a sense of mental resilience as we allow thoughts and feelings to come and go. For example, even though there is a thought that has arisen that is discomforting, we allow this to be, recognise its value in trying to provide us with information, wisely accept the message and let go of it, moving onto the next moment. We have given the thoughts ample space and attention in our subjective experience and now we can let them go, and this in itself soothes our inner experience ready for the next ones.

Step 5. Turning Equanimity Outwards

Figure 6.5: Everyone has their own unique sponge-like minds.

Do you find it easy to be compassionate towards those you like? Why? Do you find it easy to be compassionate towards those you find neutral? Why? Do you find it easy to be compassionate towards those you dislike or have a strong aversion towards? If not, what strategies have you developed that enable you to work with these people?

With this step of turning equanimity outwards, we recognise that the categorisation and judgement process is happening inside other people as well as within ourselves. For example, look at the figure. It is clear everyone has their own unique sponge-like minds and who knows their circumstances? Other people also behave based on their own unique sponge-like minds! By understanding this, we can extend our compassion not only to the people we like, but also to those who we dislike or are indifferent to. This is because we have no idea how much they identify with their own thoughts and how much thinking and feeling dominates them. It is helpful to extend compassion regardless of how similar or different we are because this aids our own wellbeing and may contribute to another person's wellbeing: 'I am really going to make more of an effort with my friend and help him when I can,' 'I understand how people might turn things into phobias and carry with them fear of certain activities so I will try to help them and not make fun,' or 'The sweater is grey and actually, if you look closer, it looks nice: I wonder why I find grey dull?'

Step 6. Extending Compassion

Figure 6.6: Extending the light of compassion.

Breaking down the prison-type walls of what we regard as good or bad, or right or wrong, is tough because these feelings relate so closely to our sense of self. While we each have unique minds that experience the world differently, we all want to be happy and not be in pain. Freedom from cognitive rigidity and relating to our own mind as an open and spacious arena rather than as a fixed sense of self allows us to shine a compassionate light (see the shining lightbulb image!) onto ourselves and others through mindfulness, helping us to acknowledge our shared humanity and extend compassion towards our friends, enemies and strangers. 'All people feel nice when they hear nice things: I will try to say as many nice things to people for the rest of this day.' 'All people suffer from fears and have had worrying past experiences of some form. So I will be kinder to those people and be patient with their idiosyncrasies.' 'All people have different tastes and the sweater is warm and functional – and who am I to say it is dull? My taste is no better!' How might you begin to extend the parameters of your compassion?

Try an equanimity meditation (explained later in this chapter) and reflect upon how this experience was for you. What did you find difficult?

Step 7. Creating a new relationship with yourself

Figure 6.7: Creating a new relationship with yourself.

Through our mindful equanimity practice, we can regulate our emotions, protect ourselves from anxiety and depression, and actively cultivate positive mental states. For example, the person in the image holds the umbrella of mental protection to use when required and is, in turn, ready to flourish like the growth of a flower. This is how mindfulness can be extended to offer therapeutic benefits in creating a new relationship with ourselves. This is the true meaning of accepting things non-judgementally. Instead of not 'judging the judgements', we can turn towards our judgements and dissolve them with wisdom, self-compassion and compassion for others.

Who are we if we are not our likes or dislikes? Our beliefs and values? Who are we if we are not our thoughts? Experiences come from our past; they have been built from childhood and they do not need to define us. I can learn from the great conversation and why I liked it so much, laugh at the swimming incident, and observe my reaction to the sweater. When things arise in our consciousness, we can label them from a wise perspective without being overly involved in them.

Case Studies

These case studies show how the seven steps involved in creating an inner and an outer equanimity can be applied to everyday situations. These case studies explore a negative, a neutral and a positive situation.

A negative situation: Tim

Tim applies for a job he has more than enough qualifications and experience for. He is sure he will get it and excitedly tells his family and friends about the interview. Unfortunately, Tim does not get the job, and this creates a number of negative feelings for him.

> Tim recognises in himself that this is a feeling of 'dislike'. In fact, his self-esteem, confidence and self-worth take a huge knock. He recognises that all his feelings are negative and heavy and there is a great deal of emotional pain associated with the experience.

> Tim recognises that he has suffered a great deal because of this experience, but what is making it worse is all the mental stories he finds himself going over in his head. He recalls past experiences of rejection; those times when his parents questioned him about if he was ever going to make something of himself. The thoughts that have emerged, such as 'you're useless' and 'try for something easier because you're no good' have begun to circulate in his mind. He sees that his mind has identified with this negative experience.

> Tim's wise mind begins to counteract. He thinks to himself, 'This is just a tiny moment in the entirety of my life. It has come and gone, and this feeling of negativity too will dissipate.' Tim understands why he is feeling this way and recognises that his mind has labelled and identified with a bad experience and now a host of other negative things are trying to creep in. But his inner wisdom tells him it will pass. So while acknowledging what is happening, he lessens his identification with this process and keeps it in perspective. This makes it pass quicker and easier.

> Tim's wise mind accepts what is happening. He stands up to what is happening not by blocking it out but by acknowledging what is occurring. He knows he is bigger than his thoughts and disentangles himself from the sticky negativity cycle that has begun to happen. Tim is totally accepting of what has happened.

> Tim thinks to himself that he is glad someone got the job and he rejoices in their good fortune. He hopes it turns out well for them and that they are able to have a great impact. Tim acknowledges that every human in the world must go through the same highs and lows of life and begins to remember that everyone is deserving of compassion.

> Tim considers that so many people in the world do not even have the opportunity to apply for jobs so, from that perspective, he is extremely lucky. He wishes everyone in the world was able to get the jobs they really wanted as he knows this would make people happy.

> Even though this was a negative experience, Tim has reframed it into a positive one. With the wisdom of knowing that things are continually changing, the wisdom of understanding how his mind tried to make it all worse, and the wisdom of the human condition, Tim feels as if this experience has given him greater resilience to respond to whatever life throws at him. He can now embrace all things that happen to him; he accepts, turns towards his judgements and dissolves them with wisdom and compassion.

A neutral situation: Amal

Amal orders some food at the staff canteen and gets chatting to Ben, who has just started working there. It was a neutral experience.

> Amal recognises that this is a judgement of 'neutrality'. This was neither a positive nor a negative experience.

> Amal recognises that his mind has labelled it as such because Ben did not say anything he particularly enjoyed or found interesting, nor was he rude or said anything controversial. Amal recognises that his mind is hardly disturbed by this experience and recalls all the other times during the day that have left him with a familiar sense of neutrality.

> Amal's wise mind begins to rise. He thinks to himself, 'This fleeting moment is like so many other neutral moments. It has come and gone, and this feeling of neutrality too will dissipate.' Amal understands why he is feeling this way and recognises that his mind has labelled and identified with a neutral experience and now a host of other neutral things are trying to creep in, even feelings of boredom. A feeling of dissatisfaction begins to arise. But Amal's inner wisdom tells him it will pass. So, while acknowledging what is happening, he lessens his

identification with this process and keeps it in perspective. This also makes it pass quicker and easier.

> Amal's wise mind accepts what is happening. He stands up to what is happening not by hiding, but by acknowledging what is occurring. He knows he is bigger than his thoughts and disentangles himself from the sticky neutrality cycle that has begun to happen and that has also begun to rewrite it as a negative experience. Amal is totally accepting of what has happened.

> Amal thinks to himself that he is glad he met Ben, that he seemed a nice person and that he hopes he has a close circle of family and friends.

> Amal acknowledges that every human in the world must go through the same neutral experiences in life and begins to think that everyone is deserving of compassion.

> This was a neutral experience, which Amal has reframed into a positive one. With wisdom that things are continually changing, wisdom of how his mind tried to make it all worse and wisdom of the human condition, Amal has turned a neutral situation into a good one. He has greater resilience to whatever neutral experiences life throws at him. He is now able to embrace all the things that happen to him, he accepts his judgements and dissolves them with wisdom and compassion. He develops a curiosity towards ordinary events and doesn't take everyday experiences for granted.

A positive situation: Irene

Irene wins some money at a local event and is really pleased. Irene regards this as a pleasurable situation.

> Irene recognises in herself that this is a feeling of 'like'. In fact, she loves it, as she hardly ever wins anything, and it has given her a rush of excitement and adrenaline. She recognises that all her feelings are positive.

> Irene recognises that she has really benefitted from winning this money and recalls all her past experiences of success. Her inner voice begins to say, 'you deserve this,' and 'this is because you are a nice person.' She sees that her mind has identified with this positive experience.

> Irene's wise mind begins to assess the process. She thinks to herself, 'This is just a tiny moment in the entirety of my life. It has come and gone, and this feeling of positivity too will dissipate.' Irene understands why she is feeling this way and recognises that her mind has labelled and identified with a good experience and now a host of other positive things are making an inner appearance. She momentarily embraces all this, as feelings of pleasure are nice, and so she grants herself time to indulge. Eventually, her inner wisdom tells her it will pass, so not to cling to it as this will in turn create a negative experience once the feeling has run its course. So, while acknowledging what is happening, she lessens her identification with this process and keeps it in perspective.

> Irene's wise mind accepts what is happening. She embraces what is happening not by overindulging, but by acknowledging what is occurring. She knows she is bigger than her thoughts and disentangles herself from the sticky positivity cycle that has begun to happen. Irene is totally accepting of what has happened.

> Irene thinks to herself that she is glad this happened to her. She wishes everyone else could feel the same things she felt. She acknowledges how nice it would be to live in a world where everyone felt pleasure, excitement and happiness. She knows the good feeling will dissipate and hopes everyone finds the strength to let go of a nice thing.

> Irene also thinks about the many people in the world who do not even have the opportunity to apply for raffle tickets, have no money and few possessions. Some even live on the streets. She is extremely lucky. She wishes everyone in the world could have enough money to be happy and content.

> This was a positive experience, and Irene has reframed it into a meaningful one. With wisdom that things are continually changing, wisdom of how her mind tried to make it over-the-top and wisdom of the human condition, Irene has managed to make a good situation better. Irene is able to embrace all things that happen to her without clinging onto the good ones; she accepts, turns towards her judgements, and experiences and dissolves them with wisdom and compassion.

Case Study: Sarah

Cultivating mindfulness and equanimity in daily life can affect our judgements and prejudices, as we are able to understand that developing positive thoughts increases our own wellbeing and leads to greater social harmony. Without mindfulness and equanimity, our judgements can lead to personal unhappiness and cause problems for others.

The practice of equanimity with mindfulness is essentially social education. Equanimity requires two complementary strands: turning inwards to observe what's happening with the mind, and then utilising this practice in everyday situations so we can put equanimity into practical use. It is not enough to just meditate on equanimity, and it is too difficult to just apply it to life without meditation. It is through the combination of both strands that we can change deep-seated habits. Think of it as preparing the soil (the mind) and then planting new behaviours. The more we water and nourish the mind by meditating and planting these new behaviours, then the more natural equanimity becomes in our lives and before we know it, we have a beautiful garden.

As you read the case study, we will first consider our own responses to it, and then consider the responses of Sarah, the subject of the case study.

Background

Sarah is 21, White British, and grew up with parents who were politically far-right. She often overheard criticisms of 'foreigners' and strong views on the state of the country. At school, Sarah had friends who shared similar views. In fact, most of the area in which she grew up seemed to share these views, and she would often see the British flag waving out of bedroom windows or from cars.

In order to fit in and gain attention and praise from the people close to her, Sarah developed a superior attitude towards foreigners and became very opinionated, often making inappropriate jokes and being quite vociferous with her opinions. Sarah was expected to provide maintenance for her family but could not find any employment, which often led to tensions at home.

On a night out with friends, Sarah had a bit too much to drink and an argument started with a group of people who looked different to Sarah. Sarah began to rant and shout at some people sitting opposite her group because they looked different and they were 'taking British jobs'. Sarah enjoyed her friends laughing and felt a surge of energy in her voice. A heated argument began. Things developed and eventually Sarah hit a young girl named Salissa in the face, causing her to become unconscious and be rushed to hospital.

Developing compassion with equanimity for Salissa

The nature of the argument was about looking different and job security: Salissa was on the receiving end of extreme views about her ethnicity and value in society. In this instance it is easy for us to develop compassion for Salissa, especially if we do not condone any form of violence towards another person.

Even if we share similar views to Sarah, we could perhaps still not condone the violent behaviour and blame it on alcohol. Regardless of our own views, we can all develop compassion for Salissa based on her experience of physical violence.

Developing compassion with equanimity for Sarah

Developing compassion for someone who we may perceive as the perpetrator of a crime is a bit harder. Because of the information presented to us about Sarah's history, we can, to a degree, develop an understanding of why Sarah holds such views (the conditioning of her upbringing and repeatedly hearing similar views by her parents and community over time). Her desire to fit in and make friends at school to form social bonds and connection seemed to rely on the foundation of these views as a vehicle towards friendship. Also, Sarah is expected to provide income for her family, yet faces the stark reality of being unable to get a job, which no doubt causes her frustration, loss of hope and perhaps a deep-seated resentment at the perceived 'cause' of her lack of employment.

However, despite knowing Sarah's background, we may still struggle to feel empathy and compassion for someone with whom we don't share similar views. We are faced with suspending our judgement and trying to be compassionate towards Sarah, even if this makes us feel uncomfortable. We can recognise that it is our own judgements about the scenario that are causing this 'blockage' of compassion. If we feel strongly about hate crimes, or violence, Sarah may have already become lost in our compassion arena and in fact could become, in our own minds, a figure towards whom anger or hatred is directed. In order to work with this, we need to look at how our own judgement comes into play and shapes our own mind.

Sarah starts off as a neutral person to us. She is neither likeable nor unlikeable because she is simply a name in a story. As the story emerges, we see Sarah as a victim, if you like, of her own circumstances; perhaps we feel a sense of sympathy with her at not being able to find a job and income for her family This perhaps makes Sarah likeable. But then her confrontational and rude behaviour may not align with our own moral code of conduct and this potentially cements feelings of dislike for Sarah, or leaves us partially confused in processing all our judgements!

In order to understand the process of our mental formations – from neutral, to liking, to disliking in the Sarah scenario – it is useful to be clear about how the mind changes and forms the judgements which then justify our thoughts, words and actions. This is where the practice of equanimity enables us to see how we can modify these tendencies, leading to less judgement and a more equanimous and compassionate view of all involved.

We recognise the trail of how our mind is shaped by our discrimination faculties and that at each stage of the unfolding scenario we hold different feelings towards Sarah. Then we can see that our feelings come from our own judgemental blueprint because of how we have been brought up, our friends, our society and culture, and so on. Then, we allow these feelings to sit there without acting upon them. We become non-reactive towards them, and because of our wish to develop compassion, we cut through the story with wisdom. We are compassionate to ourselves because we are embracing our own views, not turning them off like a tap. And we are compassionate towards Sarah because we recognise how she might have come to act the way she did.

How Sarah might have acted differently with mindfulness and equanimity

Mindfulness invites us to remain present and in a heightened state of awareness towards both our inner and external worlds. Despite Sarah's parents and friends holding strong views, by practising mindfulness Sarah could have developed an accepting attitude towards how those around her live and behave. The views of others do not necessarily need to cause Sarah any insecurity for not holding the same views, nor does Sarah need to act in ways that do not feel authentic to her. Thus, those around her do not need to influence her and Sarah's mindfulness enables her to be aware of how those opinions affect her internally, yet provide her with a non-reactive ability to simply be with those opinions and nothing more. Sarah develops equanimity with those around her because she is neither swayed by those opinions nor emotionally provoked by them. She develops self-confidence about her beliefs and behaviours due to an understanding of her internal mental habits. Or, if she is provoked by them, then, with awareness, she allows her own emotions to pass because of her understanding of the bigger picture.

She observes that her family and peers are eliciting those views and behaviours because of their own conditioning, and thus they are not a fixed reflective state of who they are. She is in balance with her circumstances and free to develop her own moral code of conduct. She finds equanimity with her employment situation as she is in a similar position to thousands of other people and her not getting a job yet is not a reflection of her self-esteem or likeability. She strives for a job but is not desperate and over-emotional if one does not arise. Sarah recognises that alcohol feeds into deep-seated habits and recognises that although she has found herself with a strong view and involved in an argument, rather than seek to blame the other person because of her own projection, Sarah feels equanimity with Salissa because she knows nothing about her or her own struggles. In any situation, we will not always be privy to the full picture, and activating equanimity in our minds is the best way to guard against an incorrect painting of the picture. Sarah labels her anger, understands why it is there and lets it go. She understands common humanity: that all humans possess the wish to be happy and everything is an expression of their own unique circumstances. Sarah realises that her upbringing and emotional tensions throughout the day have caused her to feel particularly volatile that night. She lets this feeling go because she wishes to develop compassion for herself and also for the stranger Salissa, regardless of how much Salissa may or may not have provoked her. And, like a stone dropped into a pool of water, her positive attitude and behaviour ripples out to her friends and family members, decreasing their own prejudices and judgements. Her behaviour is observed by her family members. The way they see her, think about her and communicate with her is affected. Their expectations all shift. The way they behave towards her changes, as does the way they think and behave towards others. This is the web of interconnection that occurs and why each and every one of us plays a huge role in the world. Because we are all interconnected.

Cultivating Equanimity through Meditation

The G.I. Joe fallacy (developed by Laurie Santos at Yale University) is the idea that 'knowing is half the battle' (which was the belief of the cartoon character G.I. Joe in the 1980s).[40] When it comes to the cognitive biases that shape human behaviour, knowing is not enough: it is at best perhaps one-tenth of the battle. Just because you know about the barriers to equanimity does not mean you will not experience them as soon as you encounter them. Therefore, you must also work on an experiential level, such as by cultivating a formal meditation practice. You must work on the habitual tendencies within your mind by practices such as meditation in order to alter them over time.

Through meditation, you can actively generate an equanimous mind. You can use numerous meditation techniques to do this. Here, I share a couple of helpful practices you can try to help you get started.

The Mahayana friends, enemies and strangers meditation

Mahayana Buddhism refers to one of the major traditions of Buddhism. This meditation is particularly helpful for manifesting an equal attitude towards people. You work with all three levels of people you 'like', 'dislike' and feel 'neutral' towards so you can practise compassion on all three. This really helps bring out your feelings for people and then guides you in how to reduce bias and treat them all in the same loving manner.

1. Sitting or lying somewhere comfortable, mindfully take a few breaths, cultivating a sense of stillness and peace.
2. Imagine someone you like in front of you. Make them as vivid as possible and then imagine sending these four statements to them: 'May you be happy. May you be well. May you be at peace. May you receive everything you wish.'
3. Then repeat this process for someone you do not know (neutral). This could be someone who served you food, sold you something or simply passed you in the street. 'May you be happy. May you

40 Santos, L. (2018) What is the GI:Joe Fallacy: The Science of Wellbeing by Yale University. YouTube. Available at: https://www.youtube.com/watch?v=GimHHAID_P0.

be well. May you be at peace. May you receive everything you wish.'

4. Then finally repeat this process for someone you do not like or that is causing you difficulty at this time. This may be more difficult for you and evoke uncomfortable feelings, so you may wish to choose to imagine someone you are not directly involved with, such as a character from a film or a political leader. 'May you be happy. May you be well. May you be at peace. May you receive everything you wish.'

5. Finally, imagine these three people in front of you and repeat the statements to each one indiscriminately. Then gradually expand this to your community, social world and the entire world. You can even include all animals and nature; however expansive you wish to be!

Tonglen meditation

Tonglen is a Tibetan Buddhist meditation practice of taking and giving that can be easily adapted for equanimity.

1. Sitting or lying somewhere comfortable, mindfully take a few breaths, cultivating a sense of stillness and peace.

2. Imagine someone you like sitting in front of you. Imagine breathing in all their suffering (this could be an illness or a hard time they are going through) as a form of suffocating black smoke. Then imagine replacing this by breathing out a soothing, pacifying white smoke symbolic of love, peace and calm.

3. Then repeat this process for someone you do not know, perhaps a fellow commuter, or a shop worker.

4. Then finally repeat this process for someone you do not like or that is causing you difficulty at this time. (If this is too difficult for you, evoke an imaginary person.)

5. Finally, imagine the people whom you like, dislike and whom you do not know sitting in front of you and repeat the process to each one indiscriminately. Then gradually expand this to your community, social world and the entire world.

You can also do Tonglen on yourself as a great way to foster self-compassion. Imagine yourself in front of you at a particular time that was causing you difficulty and repeat the meditation. Renowned Buddhist nun Pema Chödrön asks us to practice Tonglen on the spot, applying it to everyday life situations. By meditating, the mentality and attitude of equanimity runs deep into your consciousness and reminds you to be more mindful.[41]

Takeaway Points:

> Follow the seven steps to create an equanimous relationship with yourself. This gives you an intellectual understanding of equanimity.
> These seven steps can be applied in daily life – take the case studies as examples.
> Practice equanimity meditations to solidify equanimity on an experiential level.

41 Chödrön, P. (2002) Tonglen on the Spot. *Tricycle*. Available at https://tricycle.org/magazine/tonglen-spot/.

Chapter 7: From the Personal to the Political

So far, you have learnt about equanimity, read examples and practised meditation, and now it is time to expand equanimity to the next level.

Ron Purser's book *McMindfulness* did a great job of throwing everything up in the air and criticising the multi-billion-dollar mindfulness industry.[42] We can now drink 'mindful tea' in our 'mindful cafés' while the 'mindless homeless person' lies across the street. The juxtaposed reality of socio-economic decline is striking, whether we are in the midst of a mindful revolution or not. The promise of a mindful and compassionate society is perhaps wishful thinking in an overwhelming and negative world.

The big question becomes, has mindfulness got enough in its armoury for social change, or has it become too mainstream? Perhaps a new form of social activism that aligns with mindfulness for both the individual and the 'other', while simultaneously kicking back against socio-economic inequality, is the way forward: a three-way agreement between the individual, other people and wider society.

Looking for Calm in a Political Storm

Perhaps the first place to look for a shift from mindfulness to social activism is politics. We all have opinions about politics. Perhaps you would disagree, but the chances are you have an opinion about political leaders, Brexit, state benefits and social welfare, the fast food industry, climate change... the list could go on! Even if you would class your interest in politics as 'politics with a little p', your opinions are political by default.

Whether you class yourself as a political expert or not, you may still be searching for answers; the search for 'rightness' and 'wrongness' will continue. And perhaps there are times when you decide to deploy neutral feelings towards politics as a self-defence mechanism so you can focus on other things – or maybe you just need a rest. When we are not seeking to hang our allegiances to an external mast, the quest to be liked and the aversion to being disliked will continue into the world of our own 'mini-politics', too – our own miniscule ecosystem of truths.

One thing to be wary of is that all political ideology assumes that human disharmony lies in external conditions and seemingly relies on

42 Purser, R. (2019) *McMindfulness*, Repeater Books.

energy from an external source. While an ideology that aims to redress inequalities and improve living conditions is no doubt a worthy pursuit, this should not supersede the inner work that is also required of its supporters. Perhaps it is too easy for us to focus our attention on a specific political party as being the source of all ills – and this diversion of our attention towards this easy moral 'win' may mean that we don't fully examine our own inner failings. Perhaps this is to spare its followers the challenge of a confrontation with their inner capitalist. The word balance comes to mind.

It may also be damaging to invest so much time in external forces. Blindness in political vision or faith in science renders individuals as participants, whose defects and malfunctions can be eliminated and whose lives are managed from 'cradle to the grave'. This allows both the left and the right to shift responsibility to the other, because they believe we have to vote for one side or the other. Equanimity is significant given the continual effort required for introspection, and it places a cautionary hand on our shoulder to ensure we are not becoming too addicted, distracted or emotionally pulled in either direction.

If we disregard social ills to the role of the state then we ignore our own responsibility by continually looking outside for problems. This is not to suggest we become passive observers, but just that we balance our energy between trying to solve the world as well as find answers within ourselves. If we wish to bring mindfulness into an arena for social change, it is up to us to go deeper within ourselves. For that we need equanimity. With equanimity, we can evaluate the facts with caution and composure, and react based on a deeper understanding and evaluation of actual policy principles rather than on our instant emotional response to a well-presented idea that may be all style, but no substance.

This will help us in the world of emotional inflammation and arousal-seeking forces. With the advent of technology-based connections, there is also the very real principle of emotion-based reactions to contend with, and this is very much the case in the political arena. Various factions depend on emotional responses in order to garner support for their causes. This is a huge worry when taking into consideration branding and marketing and how these condition the brain to seek out instant gratification and dopamine hits. (Dopamine is a type of neurotransmitter and plays a role in how we feel pleasure.) For example, consider a political election campaign: it is not uncommon to find ourselves becoming addicted to social media in a bid to refresh the news, receive the dopamine hit and repeat the same process again and again, without gaining much additional insight.

Politicians seem to place an awful lot of attention on looking back at history in order to project towards a better future. It's easy to look back to correct past wrongs or continually project dreams into the future, all in a bid to achieve the worthy goals of social harmony and future peace. Yet, in the midst of this uproar, the very moment is lost. In politics, individuals are often invited to take only one of two positions (for or against), resulting in polarisation – when a more in-depth, nuanced conversation about the pros and cons of an idea may be more helpful. This is similar to the mind and its discrimination faculties (as explored in Chapter 4). Even those who are non-participants in the political process are seen as complicit (neutral) and branded as supporters of an unequal systemic structure.

Equanimity for Social and Political Change

Change can happen. If those of us who wish for social change would be willing to take on more in-depth self-analysis, mindfulness and equanimity, then change would manifest itself and ripple outwards, especially if we did this while concentrating on well-meaning grassroots-level community work (think back to Sarah's case study in Chapter 6). Then we give ourselves a chance. Collective action requires a dance between our inner selves and the outer community: a meeting of worlds rather than a division of ideas. We require action, but not from a place of division, anger or hatred. We need action to arise from an equanimous mindset.

We might never reach an end goal of equanimity, but it is a process worth investing in. Essentially, the process of equanimity must begin with establishing an equanimous mindset. Equanimity opens a space for us to pause and reflect; however, even with an equanimous mindset, divisiveness will still ensue. It is just that the people involved will be less thrown around from pillar to post by their own sense of what is right and wrong.

I genuinely believe that equanimity can take centre stage in the political realm, because it asks each and every one of us to monitor our own opinions: why and how they were formed. It asks us to understand ourselves to such an extent that our opinions are not harsh and demanding but contain insight and value.

There is currently a lot of emphasis on making mindfulness more socially active.[43] It is interesting to see mindfulness naturally evolving to take up this space, but it seems there needs to be a reshaping of its potential. Mindfulness is not about passivity towards the status quo, or blaming the individual over structural inequality. It requires a fine-tuning of the individual, others and wider society so that we can pay attention in the moment purposefully and non-judgementally.

Geshe Tashi (the abbot of Sera Jey Monastery in India) once told a group of us, when we asked about the 'cause of existence itself', that trying to answer a question like this can be unhelpful. For example, imagine a person with an arrow in their eye. Instead of trying to get the arrow out, we are obsessed with trying to find out who shot the arrow. Simply removing the arrow would ease suffering, but it is so easy to end up wasting time and experiencing suffering while trying to work out who shot the arrow. Aren't we asking an awful lot of mindfulness to not only offer inner peace to the individual, but also to cure society of its ills? Mindfulness is ethical by nature, and with equanimity it really enables people to work with themselves. This is a political act and an act of love.

Equanimity makes mindfulness more potent, and it gives context to the here and now. It explains why people act the way they do and calls on all practitioners of mindfulness to strive to become better versions of themselves: to understand their own likes and dislikes with a little more curiosity, and to engage in a practice that does not go against who they are, even if it may go against who they thought they were. Mindfulness teaches us that we are not our thoughts; equanimity tells us we are not necessarily our feelings, either.

Equanimity acts as a wise influence within our political awareness, encouraging a willingness to act with a moral and compassionate conscience. We become a wiser version of ourselves and, in this way, we move from the personal to the political, not only by developing our skillset but through our actions, which reverberate around us. Then, should we wish to engage in political or social activism, at least we can do so from a place of insight and calm.

---

43 Mindfulness and Social Change Network (2014) Available at: www mindfulnessandsocialchange.org.

Finding Social and Community Cohesion

Equanimity lends itself to both individual transformation (from a personal wellbeing sense) and a more compassionate outlook on a collective level (considering our world view). Our equanimity and mindfulness ripples outwards when we work with colleagues and organisations. Then we can affect change at a local and community level. Perhaps we can work with policy changes in the interests of reducing inequality, which is so important in a world currently experiencing huge amounts of polarisation. Even if equanimity simply acts as a pacifier to our own reactions on social media, it contributes towards a new political harmony: where we can shake hands with someone whose ideology we detest, yet embrace them with our equanimity.

Social mindfulness that breeds extensive self-awareness becomes a platform to mediate between the self and others – the individual and the social. In this way equanimity moves beyond mindfulness to become a more prosocial movement. In quieting the mind, we may experience a potential reordering of our priorities and an ethical shift in awareness towards the cause and effect of our actions. The true role of mindfulness perhaps mediates between individual acceptance and prosocial activism. It is a continual dance between the self and others. A dance needs two sets of eyes to coordinate the steps.

In Buddhism, mindfulness is only a segment of a much larger picture that includes the development of compassion and altruism and the ultimate evolution of our sense of self. Equanimity explores *how* our individual discrimination faculties solidify our judgements (as explored in Chapters 4 and 5), and enable us to cultivate equanimity in our daily lives (Chapter 6), which provides space for people to loosen their cognitive rigidity and in turn build on their compassion. In a bid for social cohesion, perhaps developing mindfulness and equanimity can be number one on the to-do list. Of course, society also needs practical help in the sense of civic, local and policy implementation. However, we must not forget that it is people who drive these movements, and individual equanimity is just the start.

With rising populations, pandemics and climate change, there is much that weighs heavily on our shoulders. The expansion of the internet means everyone has the potential to communicate with each other in either positive or negative ways. In order to pacify the potential for conflict, I could not imagine a safer way to mitigate against the inevitable ill-will and divisiveness of today's world than by practising equanimity: examining who you think you are and spending time experimentally lowering the walls of your good, bad and indifferent judgements. This may act as a necessary revolution against the negativity and doom-and-gloom attitudes that exist in the world. If each of us manages to pour spaciousness onto these walls, as a society we may find a kinder way of being.

Takeaway Points:

> Equanimity lends itself to a political arena given the foundational messages of equity, unity and universal compassion.
> If we want to change the world, we must start with ourselves.
> Equanimity has the power to help us evaluate our opinions and communicate more kindly, compassionately and considerately in traditionally reactive spaces, such as on social media.

Epilogue: Equanimity for the Future

The biggest way to break free from cognitive rigidity is to practice equanimity. Equanimity helps us develop an inner and outer ease with others and acts as our own mental protection. By doing this we are better equipped to deal with the tumultuousness of life, which will lead to greater confidence and a more focused and motivated way of being. In many ways, equanimity provides a link between compassion for the self and compassion for others.

We need to work on our mind's ability to maintain our attention in the present moment without distraction, so that when we visualise during meditation we do not get easily distracted – and as a result, the quality of our meditations will improve. We also need to balance between self-compassion and compassion for others. There is much research to support the fact that you need to practise self-care just as much as caring for others, and phrases such as 'you cannot pour from an empty cup' highlight the idea: as a loving person, if we do not start with ourselves then what exactly are we pouring? When we are equanimous, we have reached an inner understanding of who we are, why we are the way we are, and how the way we are may impact others. Loving ourselves, for all our flaws, beauty and everything in-between, is a vital first step in turning our goodness outwards. We may not be the finished article, and perhaps we never are. But at least we know our limitations and, rather than pretend these don't exist, we work on them.

Freedom of expression has taken on a new meaning because of its ease and lack of consequence (such as access to social media at our fingertips). Comments that contain either personal or social divisiveness are not vetted, and harmful remarks often become commonly accepted. Social media users seek to shame others with a moralising political discourse, so it seems more than ever that we need a universal language of self-development and an inner conviction towards a healthy transaction between people, as well as a fusion between the fulfilment of both inner healing and outer authenticity. Through compassion for the self and others, equanimity merges our inner world with how we authentically express ourselves.

To maintain inner and outer balance, we need some practical steps to take. What follows is a list of summarising points that you can take away from this book while you are seeking this balance.

1. Mindfulness has done amazing things and will continue to do amazing things, but let's not pretend it's the saviour of humankind. We do need to avoid becoming 'breath junkies'!

2. Develop equanimity with a conviction to examine your true nature – who you are, what you think and feel – and with a view to tapping into your judgemental and discriminatory mind.

3. Practise mindfulness and equanimity with the intention of being the best possible version of yourself.

4. Practise self-compassion in order to view yourself in a kinder way. Don't beat yourself up if you discover that you have a particular judgement or prejudice that bothers you – instead, work with it if it is a core belief you wish to change.

5. Practise extending the parameters of your compassion by extending love to your friends and the people you dislike, as well as strangers.

By following these steps, we are establishing an equanimity mindset: one that is more spacious, open and relaxed, and less fragile. Even if we find it hard and may not taste the true nectar of equanimity as a more permanent state, at least we are giving ourselves a fighting chance.

If you'd like a quick recap of this book in pictorial form, here is a figure capturing the entire journey!

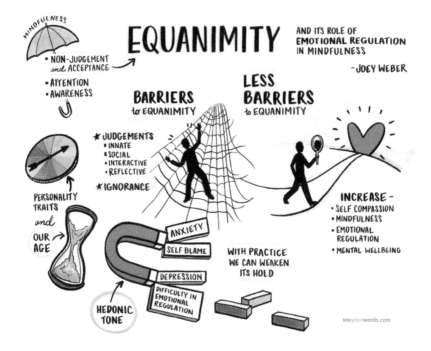

Acknowledgements

I would like to thank Willem Kuyken, Lama Jampa Thaye, Robina Courtin, Rachael Taylor, and Shamash Alidina for providing me with invaluable feedback and recommendations. Without their expert guidance and support, this book would not be what it is. I would also like to acknowledge the hard work of Kerry Laundon and Rachael Chilvers, who edited this book. They returned it so much better than when they received it! I would like to thank Clara Gispert (cover design) and Jo Byrne (all images in the book except the Shamatha painting) for their graphic expertise! I would also like to thank my mother Ondy Willson, who offered some valuable insight and who brought me to the mindfulness banquet in the first place. She trained me in mindfulness as a secular practice through her Mindfulness-based Mind Training programme, which set light to the kindling of my fire for mindfulness as a Western practice. I would also like to thank my father Andy Weber, whose infamous Tibetan Buddhist iconography (see the Shamatha image in Chapter 1) continues to stir the hearts of many, including my own.

About me

I didn't know what to do when I grew up, and maybe I still don't – but my journey has shown me the value of a varied education! I have always been very existential and concerned with meaning and purpose. My parents fell in love with Buddhism in India in the 70s, gave up everything and moved into a Tibetan monastic community when they returned home to the UK, where I grew up. It was a slightly hippy vibe, and a bunch of Westerners lived and worked there in exchange for teachings, pujas and cups of Tibetan butter tea. My formative years no doubt scaffolded my interest in meditation, even though I probably hated it at the time! Now, I love it!

I took a gap year when I finished college, which included receiving teachings from the Dalai Lama in McLeod Ganj, India, and it was here that I made a strong commitment to be of service to others. Once back in the real world, I studied Applied Social Sciences at the University of Cumbria, which enabled me to explore my fascination with human behaviour from both a psychological and sociological perspective. After I graduated, I still didn't know what to do, so when one of the tutors encouraged me to take a JNC Level 6 Youth and Community postgraduate course, I decided to give it a try. After this, I started teaching youth work at apprenticeship level for a charity and became a qualified teacher too – and I began to see the doors that different qualifications could open. With a thirst for more knowledge, I enrolled on an MA in International Development Management at the University of Manchester. While studying for this, I got a job teaching at the University of Bolton and it was then that I was offered the opportunity to complete my PhD alongside my lecturing responsibilities. It's funny how I did everything to follow a more traditional path, but 20-odd years later I seem to have ended up back on the meditation cushion.

I have a passion for mindfulness and meditation, enjoy football, support Manchester United and love an occasional pint of beer, especially after a hot sauna. I am a hybrid of mindfulness and mindlessness, but I am completely committed to self-development and walking that tightrope between the two.

After researching equanimity for many years, I have started a business, Equanamee, with a wish to spread my equanimous message.

Lightning Source UK Ltd.
Milton Keynes UK
UKHW021230180821
388987UK00007B/186